By the Same Author

Face of North America
Living Earth
The Atlantic Shore (with John Hay)
The Forest
The Insects
Ecology
Land and Wildlife of North America
The Story of Life
The Story of Butterflies and Other Insects
The Story of Dams

The Land, Wildlife, and Peoples of the Bible

Illustrations by Harry McNaught

THE LAND, WILDLIFE, AND PEOPLES OF THE BIBLE

by Peter Farb

Harper & Row, Publishers, New York, Evanston, and London

for: Mark
Thomas
Ian
Susan
Andrew

Contents

THE HOLY LAND

MEDITERRANEAN SEA

Nile Delta

Alexandria

Ramses

GOSHEN

Sea of Reeds

Pyramids

Memphis

E G Y P T

Nile River

CYPRUS

Gebal (now Byblos)

HITTITES

Sidon

Lebanon Mts.

Mt. Hermon

Damascus

Tyre

Dan

PHOENICIA

Sea of Galilee

GALILEE

A M O R I T E S

Mt. Carmel

Nazareth

Megiddo

Jordan River

Shechem (now Nablus)

SAMARIA

Shiloh (now Seilun)

GILEAD

Jordan Valley

PHILISTIA

Gibeon

Bethel

Joppa (Jaffa)

Jerusalem

Jericho

Ashdod

Bethlehem

Bethany Beyond Jordan

Ashkelon

Gath

JUDAEA

Mt. Pisgah

JORDAN

Gaza

Hebron

Dead Sea

Judaean

Desert

Beer-sheba

MOAB

Sodom

Gomorrah

N A B A T A E A N S

EDOM

A R A B I A N   D E S E R T

Negeb Desert

Ezion-geber (now Elath)

SINAI PENINSULA

Mt. Sinai

Gulf of Aqaba

• • • • • • • • • • • • • • • • •

PROBABLE ROUTE

OF THE EXODUS

RED   SEA

I. The Bible Lands

So small is the Holy Land that a soaring eagle, on a clear day, can see almost all of it at once. The Bible states that its boundaries stretched "from Dan even to Beer-sheba." Dan was the northernmost of the settlements, cradled on the flanks of lofty Mount Hermon. The southern boundary was the oasis of Beer-sheba, where travelers filled their leather water bags before penetrating the Negeb Desert to the south. From Dan to Beer-sheba is little more than 150 miles, roughly the same distance as New York City to Albany. From east to west, the Holy Land is even narrower. At its widest, a hundred miles lies between the Mediterranean coast and the Arabian Desert on the east. The land in which such great events took place is only a little larger than the state of New Jersey and smaller than Belgium.

This land that gave birth to our civilization is inconspicuous on a map of the world. But no other part of the world,

SALT LAKE COUNTY
LIBRARY SYSTEM
HDQTS., 80 EAST CENTER ST.
MIDVALE, UTAH   84047

square foot for square foot, has played such a historic role in man's life. From this land there flowed in all directions the ideas that engulfed the world. Here arose monotheism, agriculture, domestication of animals, a settled way of life in villages, systems of law and government.

Why was it exactly here, and not some other place, that civilization began? There are many complex explanations, but among the most important are the very facts of the geography of the Bible lands.

Look at the map on page 4 and you can see clearly that the Bible lands were the crossroads of the ancient world, where the main routes between Europe, Asia, and Africa intersected. The Mediterranean Sea, the Persian Gulf, and the Red Sea cause the continents to narrow here, and they also afford sea access to other areas of the world. All three of these bodies of water, by the way, are exceptional for one reason or another. The Red Sea really does have a reddish hue at certain times of the year, when various microscopic plants and animals containing reddish pigment float on its surface in such abundance that they color the water. The Persian Gulf contains the hottest ocean water in the world, about 96 degrees F. And the Mediterranean Sea, the third largest on the globe, is surpassed only by the Red Sea and the Dead Sea in saltiness.

The few routes that skirted the Holy Land deserts or that led through mountain passes were heavily traveled and on them converged peoples from many areas and with different ways of life. Items of trade were transported on these routes. The ancient empires that flourished and declined in the Near East—Babylonian, Egyptian, Assyrian, Persian, Greek, Roman—used these highways as battlegrounds. These were the routes, too, over which traveled something else besides trade caravans and marching armies: new ideas, new technology, new ways of life. So the first reason why civilization began here is that the Bible lands were the crossroads of the ancient world where new ideas and inventions were rapidly exchanged.

The second reason is that along these highways were fertile lands that could support very large numbers of people. There was a great deal of parched desert and many jagged mountains, but there were also extraordinarily bountiful stretches, watered by the Tigris, Euphrates, Jordan, and lesser rivers. Part of the explanation for the constant strife in the Holy Land lies in the conflict between peoples for the possession of fertile valleys. This bountiful land that sweeps in the shape of a crescent moon between the Persian Gulf and Egypt has been called "the Fertile Crescent." It was the scene for most of the events narrated in the Bible.

Third, the topography of the land itself was important. For one thing, it is rocky and hilly. That meant stone for building and a settled way of life in houses and villages. The steplike structure of the hills lent itself to terracing to conserve water and meant that agriculture could flourish. The topography also separated the people into isolated tribes, in contrast to Egypt and Mesopotamia where great river valleys made uniform empires possible.

The Holy Land's position at the crossroads of three continents makes it a meeting ground for species of plants and animals of different origins. Almost every kind of bird, for example, that inhabits northern Africa, southern Europe, and western Asia has been seen at one time or another in the Bible lands. The fauna comes from as far away as

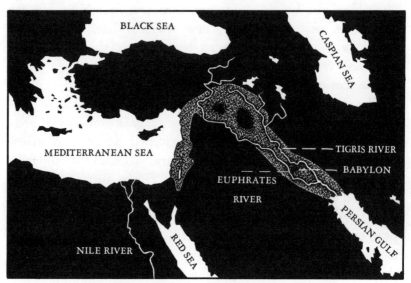

THE FERTILE CRESCENT

Central Asia (the horse), equatorial Africa (the crocodile), and western Europe (the stork).

The great variety of deserts, mountains, forests, grasslands, lakes, and seashores provides nearly every possible
habitat in which plants and animals can find exactly the
living conditions they need. About 2,250 species of trees,
shrubs, annual and perennial plants grow in the Holy
Land; Egypt, although much larger, has only 1,500. And
there are about seven hundred species of mammals, birds,
and reptiles in the Holy Land.

The contrasts in the landscape are remarkable. Mount
Hermon rises to 9,400 feet and at its summit is arctic in
climate; a little over a hundred miles away, at the Dead

Sea, the climate is tropical. In the same glance you can see
snow-capped mountains and sun-baked deserts. Alongside
cultivated fields are stark deserts that afford scarcely
enough pasturage for flocks. The Judaean Desert reaches
the very gates of Jerusalem itself. The road from Jerusalem to Jericho drops 3,000 feet in only fifteen miles, and
while fruit is growing on the farms around Jericho it may be
snowing in Jerusalem. The animals and plants, the many
different landscapes, the abrupt changes in climate—all
these things were observed by the writers of the Bible.
And they put them to use to illustrate their spiritual
teachings.

Despite the bewildering variety of landscapes, the
trained eye of a geologist detects an arrangement of the
earth of the Holy Land that is remarkably orderly. If he
were to start at the Mediterranean shore and walk eastward across the width of the Holy Land, he would detect
four parallel land formations that stretch in a north-south
direction.

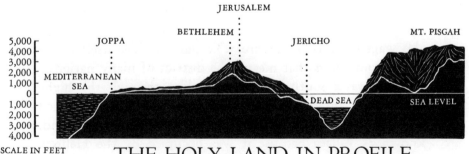

THE HOLY LAND IN PROFILE

The first of these is the level coastal plain that borders the Mediterranean Sea and extends the entire length of the Holy Land. This sliver of fertile soil was valued in ancient times for its rich harvests of fruits and grains, and for thousands of years it has been the Holy Land's breadbasket. It was valued also because of its access to the sea; on it were the Phoenician cities of Tyre and Sidon which sent out trading ships to the entire world known to the ancients. At the southern end, the coastal plain broadens out into what was once the land of the Philistines, traditional enemies of the Israelites. One name for the Holy Land—Palestine—was given it in error by the Romans. They named the whole country after the Hebrews' uncomplimentary name for the Philistines, *Pelishtim*, or "barbarians."

To the east of the coastal plain is the second north-south band, the central highlands that stretch southward from Syria the entire length of the Holy Land. In many parts of it there are forbidding mountains that rise as high as 3,300 feet, but elsewhere there are broad, fertile valleys. Galilee, where Jesus lived as a child and later preached, is such a fertile area, thick with trees and green with crops. But it is surrounded by precipitous mountains where in antiquity various groups of people found sanctuary and also waged guerrilla warfare. The name Galilee itself is derived from words that mean "the district of many nations." As you travel southward from Galilee through the highlands, you can see that the hills grow increasingly rugged and the land much drier. Finally, at the southern end, known as Judaea because it was occupied by the Hebrew tribe of Judah, the land is harsh indeed. It is covered with thorny shrubs, in some places taller than a man, that grow so close together you can scarcely penetrate them. Yet, in these inhospitable highlands, some of the most important events narrated in the Bible took place: the conquests by Joshua, the building of Jerusalem, the glories of the rule of Solomon, the birth of Jesus in Bethlehem.

The geologist, continuing eastward, can see that the slopes of the highlands plummet toward the third north-south band. This is the Jordan Valley, part of the Great Rift, which extends from Turkey deep into Africa for four thousand miles. The Great Rift is the deepest chasm on the face of the globe. The Red Sea fills part of it, and so do the elongated lakes of East Africa (among them, Rudolph, Albert, and Tanganyika). This scar on the face of the earth was not formed, as Grand Canyon was, by the gentle process of erosion. Rather, there was intermittent swelling and cracking of the earth's crust. Great blocks of land collapsed, leaving deep valleys which were flooded and in the Holy Land formed the Jordan River, Lake Huleh, the Sea of Galilee (also known as Lake Tiberias), and the Dead Sea (also known as the Salt Sea).

The Jordan has its source in springs and melting snows on the flanks of Mount Hermon. It then plunges rapidly, widening to form the Sea of Galilee, which is seven hundred feet below sea level, narrows again, and finally empties into the huge depression known as the Dead Sea. The descent of the Jordan from its source to the Dead Sea is among the most rapid of any river in the world. In approximately two hundred winding miles, it drops from several thousand feet *above* sea level to the surface of the Dead Sea, 1,285 feet *below* sea level. Hemmed in by mountain walls, the lower Jordan Valley is very much like a greenhouse from which heat cannot escape. Because conditions for life there are much the same as in the tropics, some tropical plants and animals—such as the papyrus and the crocodile—have, until recently, been found along the Jordan.

The shore of the Dead Sea is the lowest place on the land surface of the earth. This sea is also the saltiest body of water in the world—so salty, in fact, that it is impossible for a human swimmer to sink in it. During the Roman siege of Jerusalem in A.D. 70, a Roman commander sentenced some prisoners to death by having them thrown into the Dead Sea. The condemned men were thrown in from a hill, but they did not drown. Several times they were pulled out and tossed in again, yet each time they bobbed to the surface. The commander was impressed by this seeming miracle, since he did not understand its cause, and he pardoned the prisoners.

The Dead Sea is so salty because it has no outlet. The water carried into it by the Jordan and other rivers merely remains in this depression until it is evaporated by the heat and the dry air. You can see this evaporation taking place in the thick mist that lies over the surface of these hot waters. Only the water itself evaporates into mist. The dissolved minerals—ordinary table salt, as well as magnesium and calcium compounds—carried in by the Jordan remain after the water has evaporated. So concentrated do these salts become at times that a fourth of the "water" in the Dead Sea may consist of minerals. White bands of salt line the shore and chunks of gypsum have sunk to the bottom. The water is, of course, poisonous to fish and to all other living things—thus the name Dead Sea—and painful if it gets into a wound of anyone swimming in it.

The fourth, and most eastern, of the parallel bands consists of the sheer wall of hills that rises to the east of the Jordan chasm. Surprisingly, these hills are not very arid. They receive a heavy rainfall and are cut by many small streams. The explanation for the rainfall is that the prevailing winds come from the west, from the Mediterranean. These moist winds lose much of their water in passing over the central highlands, but as they cross the greenhouse of the Jordan Valley they collect moisture again and are warmed. When they strike the hills to the east of the Jordan, they are forced to rise abruptly. The clouds are cooled and the water they carry is wrung out by condensation in the form of rainfall. After passing over the high plateau east of the Jordan, the winds are completely dry. They no longer carry any moisture, and the bleakness of the Arabian Desert begins.

The climates of the Holy Land are as varied as its landscapes. There are extremes of snow and desert heat, of flood and drought, of hailstorms and sand storms. These contrasts are due in part to the conflict between the desert heat and the cool Mediterranean winds, in part to the rapid changes in the contours of the land from hills to deep valleys. In few other places in the world can such diverse climates be found in so small an area.

From May to October scarcely a drop of rain falls in most parts of the Holy Land. During the long summer drought the desert becomes a place of dry grit. Strong winds stir up dust and sand storms and often the less fearsome dust devils. Dust devils are twirling pillars of blow-ing sand, and Isaiah described them as "the chaff of the mountains before the wind . . . a rolling thing before the whirlwind" (Isaiah 17:13).*

In December, January, and February the rains often become torrential. Sudden storms may drench one area but leave another parched nearby, as the Bible points out: "I caused it to rain upon one city and caused it not to rain upon another city: one piece was rained upon, and the piece whereupon it rained not withered" (Amos 4:7). In the Second Book of Kings, the story is told of an attack by the kings of Israel and Judah upon Moab, but the two kings found themselves short of water. Suddenly, though, the streams were filled: "Ye shall not see wind, neither shall ye see rain; yet that valley shall be filled with water, that ye may drink" (II Kings 3:17). This is just what would be expected as the result of a thunderstorm some distance upstream from the valley.

The deserts of the Holy Land are in many places watered by ephemeral streams that originate on snow-clad mountains or that flow from springs. Since the rate of melt of the snowpacks varies, as does the flow from springs, these streams are often erratic—now full, now empty. Job describes the desert streams and uses them to symbolize deceitfulness: "My brethren have dealt deceitfully as a brook,

---

* *All quotations from the Bible are from the King James Version, one of the most beautiful translations and the source of many quotations in the literature of the English language for the past 350 years. After the particular book of the Old or New Testament is given, the first number refers to the chapter in that book and the second number to the particular verse or verses in that chapter. This reference, therefore, is to the book of Isaiah, Chapter 17, verse 13.*

and as the stream of brooks they pass away; Which are blackish by reason of the ice, and wherein the snow is hid . . . The paths of their way are turned aside; they go to nothing, and perish" (Job 6:15-18).

The Bible often describes cool streams, luxuriant pastures, mountains shaggy with trees. Yet the visitor today usually sees a bleak and barren landscape, the flatlands waterless and the hills bare. Almost everywhere the rocky bones of the earth show through the soil. An ancient Hebrew legend states that God had two bags of rocks when He made the world. He scattered the contents of one bag over the entire earth—but all of the other rocks in the other bag He dropped on the small area of the Holy Land.

During those centuries in which the earliest events narrated in the Bible took place, the face of the land looked much different than it does today. When farming and the pasturing of flocks and herds were in their early stages, only a small amount of land was cleared. The first step toward agriculture was the cutting down of the forests. That is what Joshua told the tribes of Ephraim and Manassah to do when they complained about the lack of farmland in the areas assigned to them: "But the mountain shall be thine: for it is a wood, and thou shalt cut it down" (Joshua 17:18).

Because of the danger in early times from wolves, leopards, lions, and other predatory animals, the flocks were not allowed to wander freely over the hillsides. Later, as the land was cleared and the predatory animals reduced in number, the flocks and herds could feed everywhere. The flocks increased tremendously and devoured any plants that sprouted from the hillsides, browsing on trees and destroying them. Soon the soil was stripped bare of its protective green covering, and it was exposed to the wind and the pelting of rain. Water washed fertile soil down the hillsides, depositing it on top of other plants farther down the slope and destroying them also. Any wisps of green leaves that groped their way out of the eroding soil were quickly eaten by the hungry animals. The soil that had once served as a sponge, soaking up rainfall, was gone and only naked rocks remained. Even before New Testament times, a dire prophecy had been fulfilled: "all the land shall become briers and thorns" (Isaiah 7:24).

There are other ways in which the Holy Land today differs from what it was in ancient times. The boundaries of nations are now, of course, different, and most of the Holy Land is divided between Israel and Jordan, with parts also held by Lebanon, Syria, and Egypt. Many of the forests of native trees are gone, but in some places new ones have been planted. Cities and villages now stand where thousands of years ago there were deserts and swamps.

But practically all of the plants mentioned in the Bible still grow abundantly in the soil of the Holy Land. Plants which appear on page after page of the Bible, plants of which the prophets and kings spoke, plants which Jesus mentioned in the parables, still can be seen. Wheat is still the staff of life, much as it was for people in biblical times. Tulips, hyacinths, narcissi, geraniums, poppies, and morning glories still sprout from the hillsides and valleys. The fruits of the Promised Land—apricots and almonds, figs and olives, pomegranates and grapes—still grow in abundance.

The birds, by and large, have endured and mighty numbers of them cleave the air. The fishes and insect legions are still present much as they were thousands of years ago. Most of the animals mentioned in the Bible can be found today, although many of them are extremely scarce. Some, like the crocodile and the lion, are now extinct there.

Much of the land and wildlife are nevertheless the same today as in biblical times. That is why visitors to the Holy Land find the Bible itself one of their best guidebooks. Of course sometimes it is difficult to determine exactly what animal or plant the Bible is describing, and in a few cases readers of the King James Version will note errors. These errors usually were not made by the original writers of the Bible, for they knew their land and its life. Rather, the books of the Bible were transmitted through several tongues and inevitably errors were made in translating them from the original Hebrew, Greek, or Aramaic languages. Most of the European translators had never seen the plants or animals mentioned, so they merely substituted the names of other living things familiar in Europe but that might never have lived in the Holy Land. Modern scientific knowledge about the conditions under which plants and animals live has enabled scholars to correct these mistranslations. At the same time, they have been impressed by the prevailing accuracy of the original texts.

The fact has clearly emerged that the Bible represents our first book of natural history in its many branches—zoology, botany, geology, astronomy, anthropology. Scholars continue to be more amazed by the Bible's accurate renderings of natural history than by its scattering of errors.

II. In the Beginning

In antiquity the Near East was a maelstrom of conflicting tribes, of clashing empires. New tribes swept out of the deserts, old empires crumbled. Amorites, Marites, Canaanites, Assyrians, Medes, Persians—these were only some of the peoples who for a time strode across the stage of the Near East. It appeared almost impossible that an independent nation could maintain itself there for very long. Yet the Hebrew nation was established and it endured longer than any other. It did more than survive. It developed a religion and an ethic that influenced all mankind.

Bible history begins in a luxuriant garden, Eden, which means "a place of delight." Eden is believed by some scholars to have been located at the eastern end of the Fertile Crescent, near where the Tigris and Euphrates rivers meet the Persian Gulf. To the people of the ancient world, this area must certainly have seemed to be an unbelievably beautiful garden. The soil was fertile and the rivers brought it abundant water. Birds and mammals in rich variety were available as food, just for the taking, and the rivers teemed with fishes. It is no wonder that the Hebrew word that was translated into Greek as Euphrates means "the luxuriant valley."

Adam was created, "of the dust of the ground" (Genesis 2:7). The name Adam is, in fact, a pun on the similar Hebrew words for "soil" and for "man." Then Eve was tempted by a serpent to taste the forbidden fruit of the tree of knowledge. Legend has it that the fruit was an apple, but nowhere does the Bible so identify it. In fact, most scholars agree that the one fruit it definitely could not have been was the apple, which was not grown in the Bible lands in Old Testament times.

The legend that the apple was the fruit on the tree of knowledge arose in the Middle Ages when artists painted pictures of Eve tasting what we know today as the apple. It probably never occurred to people who saw these paintings to question whether the apple ever grew in the Bible lands. Another source of confusion was the medieval custom of calling many different kinds of fruits "apples." Lemons were known as "Persian apples," dates as "finger apples," pomegranates as "apples of Carthage."

The fruit meant by the Hebrew word sometimes translated as "apple" was probably the apricot, which flourishes all over the Bible lands. It grows in the north and in the south, in the valleys and on the mountain slopes. A further clue comes from Solomon, who used the same word to describe a tree: "I sat down under his shadow with great delight, and his fruit was sweet to my taste" (Song of Solomon 2:3). Solomon certainly seems to be describing the apricot, for even today nomads pitch their tents under its branches to obtain relief from the sun, and it is also the fruit with the sweetest taste in the Holy Land. Additional evidence that the apricot was intended comes from Proverbs where it is described (25:11) as "apples of gold in pictures of silver." This is a remarkably accurate, as well as poetic, description of the apricot tree. Its fruit is golden, particularly when seen in the bright light of the Holy Land, and the pale undersides of the leaves look silver when they turn in the breeze.

There is no confusion about the second tree named in the Bible, the fig. After eating the forbidden apricot, Adam and Eve "sewed fig leaves together, and made themselves aprons" (Genesis 3:7). The large, tough leaves of the fig tree would certainly have made adequate clothing. Fig leaves are still sewn together in the Near East to make baskets, dishes, and even umbrellas.

In spite of its large leaves, the fig is not a tall tree, rarely growing as high as twenty-five feet, but its spreading branches provide excellent shade. In fact, its Hebrew name means "to spread out." Fig trees are abundant in the Bible lands and they have been an important source of food since the dawn of civilization. What we usually call the fruit of this tree is not really the fruit at all, but rather the fleshy receptacle in which the true fruits are imbedded. These are the gritty particles that we feel between our teeth when we eat a fig. The importance of the fig in the everyday life of ancient times is emphasized by its being mentioned fifty-seven times in the Bible.

The serpent that tempted Eve was condemned to go upon its belly, to live without legs. This is accurate zoology. Snakes developed from primitive lizards, which did

Fig

Star thistle

possess legs. But snakes developed a substitute method of locomotion—a squirming motion of the entire body—and a growth of scales on their undersides that gives traction against the ground much as tire treads do. Remnants of the hind legs snakes once possessed can be seen in the python, boa constrictor, anaconda, and several other kinds where they exist as tiny spurs that resemble thorns and are now useless for locomotion.

Adam and Eve were banished from Eden into what the Bible describes as a land of thorns and thistles. Numerous kinds of thistles grow abundantly in the Bible lands, and they can make walking extremely painful. The barbs of the thistles are the sharp leaf edges. Thorns and spines grow on many different kinds of plants, but they are particularly common on plants of the desert and semiarid regions of the world. No one is certain why so many desert plants are thorny. One theory is that they reduce the amount of water that would otherwise be evaporated through large leaves, another that they protect the plant against being eaten by animals. The theory that thorns are defensive armament seems to be supported by a close look at plants that grow in the Australian deserts. Very few of them there possess thorns, and it is significant that Australia until the importation of sheep lacked native browsing animals that might try to feed on the plants. However, other conditions must also be necessary to produce thorns, since some plants that are thorny in deserts do not put out thorns when they are grown in the humid air of a greenhouse.

The next major event told in the Bible is one of the best-known animal stories of all time: Noah and his arkful of animals that survived the flood. Noah made his ark of "gopher wood" (Genesis 6:14), which probably meant the cypress tree. This wood is extremely durable. The doors of St. Peter's in Rome are made from it and after 1,200 years they still show no sign of decay.

The Bible does not list all of the animals that Noah took with him in the ark. However, those animals that survived the flood must have been the ones that were best known to the Hebrews and that are mentioned often in the Bible.

Palestine buckthorn

About eighty species of mammals are named, about twenty-five kinds of birds, eight of reptiles and amphibians, and a dozen insects. We now know, of course, that many other living things inhabit these lands besides those named in the Bible. Yet this knowledge of approximately 125 kinds of animals reveals how remarkably familiar these ancient people were with the living things around them.

After the downpour ended and the waters began to subside, the ark came to rest against the peaks of Mount Ararat in eastern Turkey, near the headwaters of the Tigris and Euphrates rivers. All around was the hopeless desolation of a vast sea. To find dry land beyond his sight, Noah relied on a trick often used by mariners from ancient times until the invention of navigational instruments several centuries ago. Mariners used to take caged birds along on voyages. When a bird was released, the direction in which it flew showed the direction in which the nearest land lay. Jason, in quest of the golden fleece, released a dove to lead the Argonauts through the perils of a rocky coast. Columbus changed course to follow a flock of birds which he knew must eventually find land—and discovered America.

The first bird that Noah released was a raven, a large, glossy black member of the crow family, measuring more than two feet from bill to tail tip. There are several possible reasons why Noah selected the raven. First, it is a powerful flier, slicing through the air or soaring with the ease of a hawk on wings that span four feet. Second, its habitat is the mountain wilderness, and so it was just the bird to scout out any crags that emerged from the flooded earth. Most important, the raven is noted for its remarkable memory, and so this scout would not forget the location of the ark. Ravens have been trained by scientists to solve puzzles and to repeat long phrases quite distinctly, and some have even been taught to count up to seven. Ravens are still found in the Bible lands, but they have not fared as well in the presence of man as have crows. Crows are seen everywhere, but most ravens have retreated to the less inhabited and wilder areas.

When the raven failed to give Noah any inkling of land, he sent forth a dove. The Bible does not specify what kind of a dove it was, but only the rock dove and the turtledove are found in the Bible lands. ("Doves" and "pigeons," by the way, refer to the same birds. "Pigeon" is usually used for the large, chunky species of this family, "dove" for the smaller and more graceful kinds.) The rock dove is found throughout much of Europe and western Asia. It is the wild ancestor of the common street pigeon, and of the more than two hundred domesticated breeds of pigeons raised for the beauty of their plumage or for food. The rock dove was one of the earliest of all animals to be domesticated. There are records five thousand years old of man rearing them in captivity in Egypt for food and probably also as carrier pigeons. In the book of Psalms (68:13), a rock dove is described as "covered with silver, and her feathers with yellow gold." This iridescent metallic sheen can still be seen in the plumage of some street pigeons.

The turtledove is a little smaller than the street pigeon and more conservatively colored than the rock dove, with shades of gray or yellowish-brown predominating. The turtledove was never domesticated, as the rock dove was, nor is it a year-round resident of the Holy Land. The turtledove is a migrant that remains in the Holy Land from April to October and spends the rest of the year in Africa. Solomon spoke of the springtime when "the voice of the turtle is heard in our land" (Song of Solomon 2:12). He of course meant the turtledove and not the reptile, which has no voice. At migration time, almost in one day, the whole landscape reverberates with the soft, plaintive cooing of these birds, surely one of the most beautiful sounds in nature. Now the voice of the turtle is heard in North America also, for the species has been introduced successfully into southern California.

In spite of differences in size and coloration, the various kinds of doves and pigeons are essentially alike in body structure and in behavior. All are very fast fliers, and they achieve their maximum speeds only a few wingbeats after leaving a perch. Their strong wings make them capable of powerful flight in a straight line, despite storms and high winds, and some species fly many miles to obtain food for their young. They are attentive parents, and the male and female cooperate in building the nest and in incubating the eggs.

After at least five thousand years of using doves and pigeons to carry messages, man is still not certain how a pigeon "homes"—that is, finds its way back to its roost, as the biblical dove found its way back to the ark. Special senses not possessed by humans have been attributed to these birds—such as the ability to detect the earth's magnetic field or differences in air pressure—but no one has as yet proven that the birds possess these special senses or shown how they work. It is definitely known, though, that a pigeon's vision plays an important part in homing. Pigeons possess an uncanny ability to orient themselves by

Olive

remembering landmarks such as rivers, valleys, extensive forests, and mountain peaks.

The dove returned to the ark without finding land, and Noah liberated it a second time. It returned before evening, and it carried in its bill an olive leaf. This was evidence that the waters had subsided enough to expose the valleys where olive trees grow. The olive was the most important tree cultivated in the Holy Land, and it is still the most characteristic tree in the landscape: many-branched, more than twenty feet high, with a gnarled trunk and evergreen leaves. It is native only to the lands bordering the Mediterranean Sea, and it is well adapted to the conditions there. It can endure long periods of drought, and it does not require a rich soil.

A single large olive tree in biblical times provided an entire family with all of the oil it needed for food and lamps, as much as half a ton of it a year. The tree gave a year-round crop, for both the unripened and the ripe fruit are edible. The ancient farmer could gather his olive harvest whenever his work in the fields allowed time. After ripening, the olives turn black, and it was then that they usually were knocked down by beating the branches with long poles. Not all of the fruit was shaken from the tree. Some was always left on the boughs for the poor, for orphans, and for widows to gather.

So the olive leaf in the dove's beak promised a rebirth of life. Noah disembarked from his vessel with his family and he liberated the beasts of the land and the birds of the air. A magnificent rainbow spanned the sky. The rainbow is one of the remarkable phenomena that occur in the blanket of air that surrounds the earth. It is formed when the rays of the sun strike a heavy cloud of raindrops, such as remains hanging in the air after a shower. The billions of droplets act like prisms, breaking up the white light of the sun into the many brilliant colors that compose it and reflecting this whole spectrum across the sky. A rainbow is best seen when the sun is behind the person looking at it and the moisture clouds are in front. These conditions occur most often in summer when showers are localized, so that while it is raining in one part of the sky, in another it is clear enough for the sun's rays to shine through. In winter, rains usually cover a very wide area and the sun is entirely blocked out, producing no rainbow.

The rainbow symbolized the refounding of life on earth. Noah's sons became the ancestors of all humans after the flood, and the tenth and eleventh chapters of Genesis present a list of their descendants. The list is a long one, and many readers tend to skip the chapters in which it occurs. The list repays careful reading, though, for it is an excellent introduction to the various peoples known in the Old Testament world. Even more important is the moral teaching of these chapters: all mankind had a common origin in the brotherhood of Noah's sons Shem, Ham, and Japheth.

Some of the names in the list are obscure and their identification difficult, but anthropologists have been able to equate many of the names with particular peoples of the ancient world. Japheth, for example, gave his name to the port known as Joppa in antiquity and as Jaffa in Israel today. Here is where the cedars of Lebanon, imported by Solomon, were unloaded. The Javans were the Ionians, better known to us as the ancient Greeks who inhabited the Aegean Islands. The descendants of Tiras became the Thracians of northern Greece. Canaan gave his name to all of the Holy Land west of the Jordan River. Nimrod founded the Babylonian Empire. The Madai were the Medes, who inhabited the land east of Babylon and became great conquerors. The Tarshish lived in southern Spain and later carried on trade with Solomon and the Phoenicians. Heth refers to the Hittites, who erected a magnificent ancient civilization in what is now Turkey. The Jebusites held the land on which Jerusalem was later built. The Assyrians originated with Shem's son Ashur. And so it goes, name after name, a gazetteer of the biblical world.

The Bible states that the families of Noah's sons were "of one language, and of one speech" (Genesis 11:1). The story of the Tower of Babel accounts for the diverse languages later spoken. Babel was the original name for Babylon, which in Hebrew means "gate of God," referring to the gate that led to the inner city and was opened only for the New Year feast. Babylon was situated on the southern part of the flood plain between the Tigris and Euphrates rivers. It is often referred to in the Bible as Shinar (Sumer) or the land of the Chaldaeans. The builders attempted to erect a tower "whose top may reach unto heaven" (Genesis 11:4). To the ancient Hebrews this represented an impious attempt to mount into the heavens. The builders never completed the Tower since their language became confused and they could no longer understand one another.

Archaeological evidence now exists that such towers really were built. They were known as ziggurats, which literally means "houses that lift up their heads." They were erected throughout the Babylonian Empire and were probably intended as stairways by which man could ascend to meet the gods. A ziggurat somewhat resembles a pyramid, but its sides are steplike. The ruins of the great ziggurat seen at Babylon today is commonly called the Tower of Babel, but it is only a later imitation of a much earlier ziggurat. It had seven steps or stories, and it was about three hundred feet high. To us who live in an age of skyscrapers this is not a very lofty structure, but to the ancients it must have appeared to be a thrust at heaven itself.

In constructing the Tower, the builders "had brick for stone, and slime had they for mortar" (Genesis 11:3). The bricks were made from mud and the "slime" was asphalt, found all over the Iranian oilfields even today. The ancient method of construction was to lay a thin film of hot asphalt as a cement between the rows of bricks. Asphalt-covered bricks also were essential in the foundations to protect them against the dampness caused by the nearness of the Euphrates River. So solid are walls built in this way that now, thousands of years later, archaeologists have to break them apart with pickaxes during excavations. Mud bricks and asphalt formed only the interior of the ziggurat. Its outside walls were faced with glazed bricks in shining colors and a golden shrine was placed on the summit.

With the destruction of the Tower of Babel, the Bible's story of the early history of mankind ends. The stage is now set for the emergence of a descendant of Noah's son Shem: Abraham, the first great patriarch of the Hebrews. He was the man to whom God promised: "I will make of thee a great nation, and I will bless thee, and make thy name great" (Genesis 12:2).

III. A Nomad with Flocks
and Herds

On the banks of the little Balikh River in southeastern Turkey, about sixty miles north of its juncture with the Euphrates River, a traveler today finds the small mud-brick settlement of Haran. In antiquity this town was one of the most important in the Near East, a wealthy trading center where caravan trails crossed. No one would remember Haran today were it not for an event that took place there 3,900 years ago. Abraham, his wife Sarah, and his household set off with their herds and flocks on a historic journey to a Promised Land.

Until some thirty years ago little was known about ancient Haran. Some archaeologists thought it might have been a part of the ancient Kingdom of Mari, but others doubted whether such a kingdom had even existed. Then, beginning in 1933, Mari was excavated in present-day Syria. A palace of more than 250 rooms, perhaps the largest ever built in the Near East, was discovered under the rubble of ages. Mari was unveiled as one of the great cities of the ancient world. A ziggurat was unearthed, and so were 20,000 clay tablets covered with writing.

The clay tablets preserve ancient police records that refer constantly to the threats of Semitic nomads who lived on the frontiers of the kingdom and raided the towns of Mari. Some of these nomads had names that later became familiar as Hebrew names, such as Ben-Yamun (Benjamin) and Abram (Abraham). In the biblical list of Abraham's ancestors (Genesis 11:10-26), many family names are the same as those of several towns around Haran. Abraham's relatives either took their names from the towns in which they lived or else they were important enough to give their names to these towns. In any event, there can be no doubt that archaeology has uncovered at Mari the origins of Abraham and the Hebrew people.

Further archaeological evidence that Haran was the city of Abraham comes from documents of that time. They tell about the troublesome *Habiru* or *Apiru*, Semitic nomads who swarmed out of the deserts and attacked the settled communities in the Fertile Crescent. *Habiru* (or "Hebrew") was a word of disparagement, probably meaning "the dusty ones." It did not refer to the Hebrew people in particular but rather to all the land-hungry Semites who led a nomadic life. In the book of Genesis (14:13) Abraham is called "the Hebrew," and so this general name was finally limited to his descendants.

The time of the Habiru was an unsettled one in the Near East. The people known in the Bible as Amorites—that is, a group of Semitic nomads—were everywhere on the move from the desert fringes of the Fertile Crescent into Syria and Mesopotamia. Haran, in Abraham's time, had already become one of the new Amorite settlements. The Amorites swept eastward and conquered Babylon, on the east bank of the Euphrates River, which they made their capital. The sixth king in their dynasty was Hammurabi whose famous code of laws, carved on an eight-foot-high stele, or stone pillar, was unearthed in 1902 at Susa in southwestern Iran.

Abraham's journey southward from Haran led through the entire length of Canaan, through the Negeb Desert to Egypt, and finally northward again to the Promised Land. We are apt to visualize him traveling in one of those long camel caravans that can still be seen today in the deserts of the Near East. That is not a true picture at all. Indeed, it is possible that until he reached Egypt he traveled on foot, with no beasts of burden except perhaps a few asses, those long-eared members of the horse family also known as donkeys.

The Bible makes no mention at all of Abraham's departure from Haran with any beasts of burden. Beasts of burden were not common at that time in the northern portions of the Tigris and Euphrates valleys. And the first beasts of burden to be used there were not camels but rather asses. The wild ass of the Sahara Desert of North Africa was domesticated as early as six thousand years ago, but its spread eastward to Egypt and the Fertile Crescent was slow. The earliest written references to domesticated asses in the eastern end of the Fertile Crescent date from about the time that Abraham left Haran in search of the Promised Land.

The first mention of the ass in the Bible occurs when it is

stated that the pharaoh (the ruler, literally "the great house") of Egypt presented Abraham with several asses as gifts (Genesis 12:16). To the Egyptians in Abraham's time, the ass was solely a means of transporting goods. Only later was it used for riding, for pulling the plow, and for turning millstones to grind grain. There once were three kinds of wild asses native to Africa, but two of them are now extinct and only a small remnant of the third survives today under careful protection in Somalia.

The domesticated ass or donkey is one of the world's most useful animals. It goes long periods without water, works hard in hot climates, and survives on a minimum of food. Yet the donkey has also been despised almost everywhere because of its stubborn temperament. It possesses endurance and persistence, and so it makes an excellent pack animal, although it is the slowest member of the horse family. Its milk is extremely nutritious, much resembling human milk in its chemical composition. The mating of a male donkey and a female horse has produced the hybrid known as the mule, a cautious and patient animal much used even today in mountainous areas of the world. Descents into the Grand Canyon, for example, can be made on the backs of sure-footed mules.

The ass was one of the most important of all animals to the Hebrews. Numerous laws existed about the treatment of asses, which testifies to the important place they held in the Hebrew economy. An ass had to be rested on the Sabbath, and one that had fallen under the weight of its burden had to be helped. The Hebrews were the only people in the ancient world to use it for riding, although only the common people did so. It was thought humiliating for an earthly ruler to ride on an ass. Biblical kings, such as David, and other important personages are recorded as riding on mules or in chariots pulled by horses, but never on asses. So when Jesus rode on an ass, it was a symbol of his humility.

Occasionally the Bible mentions the "wild ass." This does not refer to an untamed domesticated ass, but rather to a different species altogether: the onager. Domesticated asses were African in origin, but the onager is an Asiatic horse with several donkeylike characteristics. Its ears are longer than those of a horse but shorter than those of an ass. The onager's tail is short-haired except at the tip where it ends in a brush, while the horse's tail is made up completely of long hairs. Most people in Asia today regard the onager as untamable. Pictures from the Royal Cemetery of Ur in Babylon, however, dating from about 4,500 years ago, show onagers drawing chariots. They were used for that work for only a short time. When the horse was introduced into Mesopotamia a few centuries later, there no longer was need for the onager. Because it is more docile and has greater strength, the horse is much superior.

The Bible mentions that Pharaoh also presented Abraham with camels, but most scholars believe that this word was mistakenly added by a transcriber of the original Hebrew texts at a later date. Archaeologists now know that the camel did not become established in Egypt as a domesticated animal until several hundred years after Abraham visited there. The camel was native to Arabia and the lands around the Euphrates, and it later spread westward to Egypt and the Sahara. The Bible text is undoubtedly accurate, though, when it states that Abraham's servant, sent to northern Arabia to find a bride for his son Isaac, came upon Rebekah watering her camels (Genesis 23: 24). Even though the camel had not yet reached Egypt when Abraham visited there, it was common in the Fertile Crescent.

The biblical camel is the one-humped kind, often called a dromedary. (The two-humped bactrian camel is an Asiatic animal that ranges from northern Iran across central Asia to China.) The only people in the ancient world who used the camel were those who did not have available other kinds of domesticated beasts of burden, such as asses, horses, and oxen. In many ways the camel has little to recommend it. It is a very slow breeder: a single offspring is born every three years, sometimes less often than that. The camel's ability to learn is meager, and it is impossible to train one to respond as well as a horse. It is completely untrue that a camel possesses some special sense of direction in the trackless desert. In fact, a camel easily loses its way or becomes separated from the rest of the caravan. It is generally bad-tempered, the males so much so that Roman soldiers kept them outside the walls of their posts. Camels often bite, and when angry they have been known to shower their masters with evil-smelling spit.

Camels are desirable animals only to people who inhabit deserts because they are excellently adapted to the inhospitable conditions there. A camel's nostrils are slits that can be closed to keep out dust and sand. There is a groove leading downward from each nostril to the upper lip, with the result that moisture from the nostrils is not wasted but instead is caught in the mouth. The broad and spongelike feet adapted to walking on sand, the willingness to eat practically any plant that grows in the desert, the low water requirements for long periods of time—all these things have made the camel the primary means of transportation in arid areas. In addition, camels provide milk, and their hair is woven into fabric for clothing and tents. Without camels, many desert areas would never have become inhabited by man at all.

It is true that a thirsty camel can drink enormously and fast, about twenty-five gallons of water in little more than ten minutes. It is also true that a camel can travel for a long time—about four days—without drinking. But the ability of the camel to store water has been greatly exaggerated. It is not true that water is stored in the hump, nor is very much stored in its unusual three-chambered stomach. The first, and largest, stomach has little pouches on its walls which were long thought to serve as storage tanks. Research in the past several years, however, has revealed that the total capacity of these tanks is a mere seven quarts, surely of little use to an animal the size of a camel.

The camel's hump stores food, not water. It is a mass of muscle around which fat accumulates. This fat represents reserve fuel which the camel draws upon for nourishment on a long trip. The ability to carry a food supply on its own back represents one of the main advantages of using the camel for desert travel. It can be fed at the beginning of a trip and not again until the end. Between those two feedings, it replenishes some of its expended fuel by eating dry shrubs or thistles it finds along the route. After an arduous trip, the hump is shrunken and it flops to one side. The camel then needs a lengthy period of recuperation. When the animal is rested and well fed again, the hump once more becomes erect and thick.

Biologists now know that the camel's secret weapon against the waterless desert is not storage but conservation. The camel possesses a remarkable ability to survive a severe loss of water from its blood, its body fluids, its tissues. It reduces water waste in other ways, too. Its thick wool coat provides insulation against heat, its stiltlike legs hold its body high above the hot desert sands, and it does not sweat as much as most other mammals do.

A wonderfully detailed painting of what Abraham's household probably looked like has been discovered in a prince's tomb in Egypt, dating from about 3,900 years ago (portions of it are reproduced on pages 36 and 37). It shows a family of seminomads entering Egypt (unlike true nomads, seminomads will settle down with their flocks to plant some grain when they find unoccupied fertile land). Hieroglyphics on the picture explain that they are "sand dwellers," or Semites. With careful attention to detail, the artist has pictured the arrival of the band of men, women, and children. The leader of the band is shown holding a goat and a shepherd's crook. His coat is made of brightly colored and striped material: it might possibly be a "coat of many colours" such as Joseph wore (Genesis 37:3). The men carry water in animal skins. One of them plays the eight-stringed lyre, the "harp" made famous by David. The children and the baggage are carried on asses, not on camels. The weapons are the bow and arrow, the javelin, and a heavy throwing stick somewhat like the boomerang of Australia. A gazelle is shown, possibly because it was one of the food animals hunted by the Semites. The painting makes particularly clear that there was nothing wild or primitive about these people. Their weapons, their tools, their whole way of life was beautifully adapted to traveling from place to place as they pastured their animals.

The route taken by Abraham is only sketchily outlined in the Bible, but these hints, combined with modern archaeological knowledge of ancient roads, allow us to plot it fairly well (see the frontispiece map). After Abraham arrived in the land of Canaan, he erected an altar near Bethel. The grazing lands there, however, could not support his flocks and herds. Like many nomads of that time in the Holy Land, he sought relief from drought in Egypt, watered by the mighty Nile. His route to Egypt probably took him through little Jebus, a place that later, its name

changed to Jerusalem, became the most important city in the Holy Land. He also stopped at the oasis of Beer-sheba. The names of many places in the Holy Land contain the word "Beer," which means "well" in Hebrew. Beer-sheba may mean "seven wells" in reference to the many deep wells that made this oasis possible. Beer-sheba, unlike most of the cities in Canaan, had no walls to guard it. It did not need them, for the bleak desert that surrounded it was a greater defense than any fortress.

To reach Egypt, Abraham had to cross the Negeb, which means "dry land." Today it is one of the most forbidding deserts on earth, and for a long time scholars

Egyptian wall painting from the time of Abraham, showing arrival of caravan of Semites

wondered how Abraham survived it with his livestock. Archaeologists have recently discovered that in Abraham's time the Negeb was very different from the forlorn waste it is today. Then it was dotted with oases and camps, and green with agricultural lands. The settlements were close enough for him to travel from one to another before his food and water gave out.

Archaeologists have been able to reconstruct the story of the Negeb in the time of Abraham through the study of something many people might consider an unpromising source of information—broken pottery. Pottery, made from clay and baked in a kiln, is probably the most durable thing man has ever made. Glass flakes away, metals corrode and rust, wood and fabrics are destroyed by dampness and insects. Pottery alone survives. A pottery jar can easily be shattered, but the broken pieces or shards will endure for thousands of years. Different methods of manufacture and the various designs shown on the shards give clues to when the pottery was made, who made it, and its relationship to pottery made by neighboring peoples.

Archaeologists have studied the shards discovered in the Negeb that date from about the time that Abraham crossed it. They learned that all of the pottery made throughout this vast area was almost exactly the same. This reveals to the archaeologist that those were settled times, that the people of the Negeb were in peaceful trade with one another. But the routes of trade soon came to serve as routes for invading armies. Shortly after Abraham journeyed through the Negeb, nomads poured out of the desert and laid waste the villages. The oases, the farms, and the dams built for water conservation in the Negeb were utterly destroyed. For about seventeen hundred years thereafter the land lay desolate, until the rise of that remarkable people, the Nabataeans, who occupied it in numbers reaching possibly as high as 100,000 people. The Nabataeans, however, declined by about the second century A.D. and once again the land lay idle under the winds and searing sun, until modern Israel cultivated it once more.

Many people regard the inhabitants of oases as typical desert dwellers, but actually they are not desert people at all. An oasis is a completely artificial world that surrounds a natural spring or man-made wells. The plants that grow in oases, such as figs and dates, cannot survive in the surrounding desert without the aid of man. The boundaries of an oasis usually are sharply defined. Plants grow right up to the edge of the watered area, and only a step beyond that the barren desert begins. The entire world of the oasis dweller is contained within the green borders of irrigated gardens and fields, and few inhabitants of oases venture into the desert.

The true desert people are nomads, such as the present-day Bedouins of the Negeb Desert. They travel with their flocks across the thirsty land, seeking out its scant vegetation. Their customs are adjusted to living in a world where water is a constant need. They visit the oases only to trade their sheep, goats, and camels for the grains and fruit grown in irrigated fields. On his long journey to Egypt and the Promised Land, Abraham lived more like a nomad than an inhabitant of an oasis.

When Abraham went from Egypt back to Canaan, that land was still stricken by drought. There was scant pasturage

39

for the combined flocks of Abraham and his nephew Lot, who had been traveling with him, and so they decided to separate. Lot chose to travel to the lower Jordan Valley, where he settled near the wicked cities of Sodom and Gomorrah. Soon afterward these cities were destroyed, possibly by volcanic eruptions, for the Bible attributes their destruction to "brimstone and fire" (Genesis 19:24). No one knows for certain when the last volcanic eruption took place in the Holy Land, but it may have been as recently as the Middle Ages. There are numerous references in the Bible to volcanic action, and a geologist can see clear evidence that the Jordan Valley has been a center of volcanism in the past.

It is also possible that these cities were destroyed by the igniting of a mixture of natural gas and petroleum. Geologists have very recently discovered natural gas deposits close to where it is believed Sodom existed. The ruins of Sodom and Gomorrah have not as yet been uncovered. They are probably buried beneath the silt and water at the southern tip of the Dead Sea.

Lot was warned of the impending destruction of these cities and told to flee without looking back. But Lot's wife, who turned around to view the destruction, was changed into a pillar of salt. At the southwestern end of the Dead Sea one can see what local people call "The Pillar of Salt." The pillar is about forty feet tall, and it rests on a pedestal of salt that is an additional forty feet in height. This formation was carved by rain and running water out of Mount Sodom, a gigantic salt ridge nearly seven miles long and 650 feet high. From a distance, this ridge glitters as if it were covered with diamonds. It was formed from the tremendous amounts of salt that settled to the bottom of the

Dead Sea when this sea was larger than it is today. Then pressures in the earth's crust buckled and raised these sediments as a mountain above the level of the sea. Ever since, water from winter storms has cut deeply into it, sculpturing the ridge into fantastic shapes, such as the tall, thin pillar of Lot's wife, which does somewhat resemble a human statue.

The Bible notes that Abraham was "very rich in cattle" (Genesis 13:2), and he is often described as possessing flocks and herds. In the early books of the Bible, the word "cattle" usually refers to sheep and goats rather than to the

Barbary sheep

cows and bulls we now call cattle. Cows are much more difficult to keep than are sheep and goats. They require more care, and their larger size also demands an abundant and constant food supply. Such care and a reliable food supply were available only in permanent settlements, but Abraham lived much of his life as a nomad. It is possible that he may have maintained a few cows, but they certainly were not as numerous as his sheep and goats.

Sheep and goats were the two most important domesticated animals of the Hebrews. The sheep is named more often in the Bible than any other animal—about 750 times —and the goat is mentioned nearly two hundred times. The goat may have been the earliest food animal to be domesticated by man, and that probably took place in the vicinity of Jericho about nine thousand years ago. The only animal domesticated earlier was the dog. The possession of dogs probably aided man in his domestication of the goat because they could be used to protect the herds. It was not until much later, after Joshua had conquered Canaan, that farming replaced animal husbandry as the more honored profession. Even after the Hebrews became a mighty nation under the kings, the people still recalled with longing the simple pastoral life their ancestors had lived. Throughout the history of the Hebrews, even in the glittering court of Solomon, the life of the shepherd was upheld as the most desirable existence.

Sheep and goats belong to the same family of hoofed mammals. Although zoologists recognize several differences in anatomy between them, the ancients undoubtedly were more interested in their different habits and the various raw materials each supplied. Goats feed primarily on the leaves of shrubs, sheep on grasses. Goats are thus better adapted to life in deserts where thorny shrubs grow in abundance. They can even climb trees with sloping trunks to browse on foliage too high to reach from the ground. Both goats and sheep provided meat, but the sheep was preferred for its wool, while the goat furnished more milk. Milking and making cheese and other milk products were probably first learned by men tending their goats, before cows were domesticated.

In Old Testament times practically all clothing was

Wild ancestor of goat

made from sheep's wool. We are used to seeing sheep that have been bred for their white wool, and so it is difficult for us to realize that most sheep in biblical times had a brown coat or one patched with black and white. The hair clipped from goats, on the other hand, was woven into coarse cloth, which was used to make the black tents in which the nomads lived. The size of a tent depended upon the wealth of the owner, but even the simplest tent was divided by curtains into a front room for entertaining and another room for cooking and for the children. The holy Tabernacle itself, which sheltered tablets with the Ten Commandments engraved upon them, was originally a tent.

Rich in livestock and servants, Abraham settled at Hebron in the Promised Land of Canaan. There was born to him Ishmael, who became the forefather of the Arabian people, and his beloved son Isaac, who pastured his flocks mostly in the high valleys around Hebron. Hebron is due south of Jerusalem, in the central highlands, at an altitude of about 3,300 feet. It lay astride one of the main routes of the Holy Land which passed through other important biblical towns: Beer-sheba, Bethlehem, Jerusalem, Bethel, Shiloh, and Shechem. To the east of Hebron lay the barren wilderness, to the west cultivated lands, to the south the district that became noted in ancient times for its abundance of sheep and goats. Abraham and Isaac settled in what was to become one of the most historic areas of the Holy Land.

IV. Land of the Pharaohs

Joseph, the great-grandson of Abraham, arrived in Egypt as a slave sold into bondage by his envious brothers. The Bible tells how Joseph correctly interpreted a dream and was released from prison, and how he rose to become prime minister at the court. Joseph sent to Canaan for his aged father Jacob—also called Israel, which means "God rules" —and his eleven brothers, bidding them live with him in Egypt. That is how the original Twelve Tribes of Israel were founded, and they flourished for the next twelve generations in "the land of Goshen" (Genesis 45:10). Goshen was a fertile area at the delta of the Nile River where it empties into the Mediterranean Sea. When a river carries large amounts of sediment to its mouth and there creates an expanse of new land, that land tends to be approximately triangular in shape, with its apex pointing upstream. Because its shape resembles a letter of the Greek alphabet, *delta*, Δ, that is what it is called.

Many scholars believe that Joseph was able to rise to power because he lived during the reign of the Hyksos. The Hyksos assumed power in Egypt about 3,700 years ago, and they ruled for about 150 years. They had infiltrated into the Near East even earlier than that. About four thousand years ago an Egyptian who was living in what is now Syria wrote about these people who were becoming "so bold as to oppose the rulers of the foreign countries."

The origins of the Hyksos are obscure. Their Egyptian name—actually *hyk khwsht*—means simply "rulers of foreign lands" and gives no clue as to who they were or where they came from. Some scholars believe the Hyksos were Semitic tribesmen from the Near East. If so, then Hyksos pharaohs would have had in common with Joseph many of the same customs and a similar language. It seems more probable, though, that the Hyksos arose in the area of the Caucasus Mountains in southern Russia. Whatever their origins, they adapted themselves quickly to local customs in the lands they invaded. In the Holy Land many of them took Semitic names. In Egypt they used Egyptian writing and language.

The Hyksos marched on Egypt as a well-organized war machine. The Egyptians regarded them as a barbarian horde—even calling them "shepherd kings"—but there was nothing barbarian about them. They were skilled merchants who introduced a new series of weights into Egypt and builders who developed the rectangular fortress. They even originated an advanced method of warfare:

horse-drawn chariots from which they showered the Egyptians with arrows. The Egyptians, on foot, were no match for them.

Southern Russia seems confirmed as the homeland of the Hyksos because of the horses they brought with them. Before domestication by man, there were three races of wild horses in the world. The Przewalski horse still survives in dry areas of Mongolia, although probably only a few dozen animals exist. The second kind, the extinct forest horse, was an inhabitant of the cold forests of northern Europe and Russia. The third was the tarpan, which inhabited the grasslands of southern Russia until it became extinct in 1851. The tarpan was small, gray in color, with a dark stripe from its mane to its tail—and it was from the tarpan that domesticated horses were derived.

No one knows for certain where the first horses were domesticated, but it may have been in the area of Turkestan. There the people were seminomadic, moving about to find grazing lands, but also settling down for a while to raise crops when they found patches of well-watered land. The horse gave these people great mobility for this way of life. The horse was slow, though, to reach Mesopotamia. Hammurabi, the ruler of Babylon, did not even mention it in his code of laws of about 3,750 years ago. Only fifty years or so afterward there was a stirring of northern peoples, among them the Hyksos, who moved southward and brought the horse to the entire Fertile Crescent. During the Hyksos rule in the Holy Land, horses suddenly appear in human burials at Jericho, the same sort of burial of horse, war chariot, and dead warrior as has been unearthed in southern Russia. By the time of Joseph, or a little after,

writings about horses and pictures of them became plenti-
ful in Egypt. These horses are seen to be small and graceful, much resembling today's Arabian breed. At first they
were used exclusively for military purposes in drawing the
two-wheeled chariot. By the time of Solomon they were
used as cavalry, and he had 12,000 mounted troops in addition to his 1,400 chariots.

The civilization of the Egyptians was already an ancient
one by the time Joseph arrived there some 3,650 years ago.
The first pyramid was built about 5,000 years ago. It is
known as the Step Pyramid because it rises in a series of
steps or terraces to a height of 250 feet, much like the
ziggurats of Babylon. The Great Pyramid of Cheops at
Giza, built only a few hundred years after the Step Pyramid, was the tallest structure ever erected until the 19th
century. It rises to a height of 481 feet, and its base is 756
feet square. It is composed of nearly two and a half million
blocks of stone, and many blocks weigh as much as 5,000
pounds. The blocks were cut by hand and laid in place
with an accuracy often within a hundredth of an inch of
exactness. The truly amazing thing is that this pyramid
was built with no other mechanical equipment than the
lever and the roller, for at that time the Egyptians had not
yet learned the use of the wheel. The Great Pyramid is the
sole surviving monument of the Seven Wonders of the Ancient World.

More than thirty major pyramids were built during the
thousand years before Joseph. Each one guarded the body
of a pharaoh entombed in a chamber deep inside the pile
of stone blocks. In addition, lavish tombs were cut out of

the rocks, and the most colossal temple of all time was built at Karnak. The half-lion, half-king Sphinx that crouches on the desert looking out upon the pyramids of Giza was hewn mostly from a single giant outcropping of rock. The Egyptians are thought to have carved this Sphinx as a representation of the god of the morning sun, Harmachis. The belief that it typifies wisdom is a legend that did not originate until a few thousand years afterward when the Greeks conquered Egypt.

The ancient Egyptians were able to undertake their monumental building projects along the Nile because of a unique factor—the Nile River itself. Most rivers in the Bible lands dry up during the rainless summer, but not the Nile. At its sources far to the south in the equatorial mountains, heavy rains and melting snow feed the tributaries that converge to form the Nile. The torrent of water reaches Egypt during the late summer and it overflows the banks. Each year a fresh layer of fertile moist soil is deposited along the banks, allowing the sowing and reaping of vast amounts of food.

Such an abundance of food meant that not all of the people had to work at agriculture. There was always surplus labor available for building projects. Engineers, craftsmen, and administrators were freed from the burden of manual labor and instead could devote their energies to building temples and irrigation works. It was therefore no exaggeration when the Greek historian Herodotus called Egypt "the gift of the Nile."

Along the Nile—and, in fact, throughout the ancient Near East—the most important grain crops were wheat and barley. Both grains have been cultivated in Egypt and the

Near East since man's earliest recorded times, so early that no one knows for sure when or where these plants were first domesticated. Grains of wheat have been found in the settlements of Stone Age people, long before the events in the Bible took place. The earliest evidence in the world of wheat cultivation comes from the vicinity of Mount Carmel, on the coast of northern Israel, and it dates from about nine thousand years ago. Today more wheat than barley is grown in the Holy Land, but it is believed that barley may have been the dominant crop in Old Testament times. Wheat is more nutritious, but it is a more difficult crop to grow since it requires a deep, moist soil and a long growing season. Barley, on the other hand, can survive heat and drought better than any other grain. It will grow in much poorer soil than wheat, and it does not require so long a period of time to ripen.

The Egyptian farmers obtained their harvests fairly easily, but it is obvious from many statements in the Bible that the farmer in the Holy Land lived a life of unremitting toil. When Adam was cast out of Eden, his laborious life as a farmer in the Near East was described vividly: "Cursed is the ground for thy sake; in sorrow shalt thou eat of it all the days of thy life . . . In the sweat of thy face shalt thou eat bread" (Genesis 3:17-19). There are also numerous references to the constant threat of famine (such as the one that brought Abraham to Egypt) caused by drought, hailstorms, crop diseases, or the ravages of insects.

Archaeologists have discovered an agricultural calendar scratched in limestone, dating from the tenth century B.C., about the time of Solomon. It details how the Hebrew farmer allocated all of his time (except for one short period of "festivity" at the harvest) in raising wheat and barley for bread, grapes for raisins and wine, olives for oil.

> His two months are olive harvest
> His two months are planting grain
> His two months are late planting
> His month is hoeing up of flax
> His month is harvest of barley
> His month is harvest and festivity
> His two months are vine-tending
> His month is summer fruit

In the Holy Land, barley was usually sown in the fall and gathered in the spring. Since its protein content is less than that of wheat, it was used mainly to feed animals. It was also the chief grain of the poor people, and so it became a symbol of poverty. The laborers who built the Temple at Jerusalem for Solomon had a daily ration of 20,000 measures of barley. In the New Testament we are told that Jesus fed the multitudes with barley loaves. Barley was such a staple grain of the Hebrews that it furnished them with units of measurement—3 barley grains laid end to end were equal to an inch, about 24 to a "span," and 48 to a "cubit" (about 17 inches).

When Joseph heard Pharaoh's dream about seven ears of good corn on one stalk, followed by seven ears of meager corn grains, he interpreted it to mean that seven years of bounty would be followed by seven years of lean grain harvests. Among the numerous varieties of wheat that are now grown is one kind that, as in Joseph's time, still bears seven ears on each stalk. (Wheat and barley are referred to as "corn" in the King James Version. This does not mean Indian maize, which North Americans call "corn," since maize was unknown in the Old World until Columbus discovered America.)

The Egyptians believed that the Nile would bring the gift of rich harvests only so long as their gods were worshiped. After careful study of the stars, the moon and the sun, and the planets, the priests of ancient Egypt devised an accurate calendar and learned to predict the rising of the Nile's waters. These observations of the heavens resulted in the highest achievement of Egyptian science: the solar calendar. It was brought from Egypt to Rome by Julius Caesar and it has continued in use around the world, with only minor modifications, to this day.

The Egyptians worshiped a multitude of gods. Chief among them was the sun god Ra who, in this land of almost perpetual sunshine, appeared to be the very giver of life. The Egyptians worshiped more than two thousand other nature gods: countless kinds of mammals, birds, reptiles, fishes, even trees and rock formations. Anubis, the god of the dead, was depicted as a jackal. The sacred bull, known as Apis, was believed to have been born from a moonbeam and to represent Ptah, the father of all gods and men. When the reigning Apis bull died, it was mummified and buried in a huge vault cut out of rock. The Egyptians then searched the land for a new Apis, which was recognized by a colored spot on its tongue and special markings on its back.

Thoth, the scribe of the gods, who wrote down the records of every human being, was most often shown in Egyp-

Anubis

tian pictures to have the head of a bird—an ibis. That was appropriate. The ibis dwelt among the papyrus reeds at the borders of the Nile, and the Egyptians made paper from papyrus. The ibis is large and white, with a black tail and black head, and it is related to the spoonbill of the Gulf Coast of North America. It wades on its thin stiltlike legs through the shallow water and mudflats, probing beneath the surface with its long curved bill for frogs, worms, and shellfish. There are no longer any ibises in Egypt.

Thoth

When their habitat of papyrus reeds disappeared along the Nile, the birds became extinct there also.

The papyrus reed or bulrush was one of the most abundant plants to grow along the banks of the Nile. It is tall and very graceful, bearing at the top of its fifteen-foot stem a plume of wispy stalks that resemble feathers. The papyrus could endure the rushing waters of the Nile at floodtime because its extremely large root system served as an anchor. Although the papyrus is no longer found in Egypt, it survives today in the Jordan Valley of the Holy Land and around the Sea of Galilee, as well as several other places in the Mediterranean.

Papyrus furnished the world's first material for making paper and, in fact, our word paper is derived from it. The stem was pressed flat under heavy weights until it dried. It was then cut into sheets of suitable size which were polished with ivory to make a smooth writing surface. Sometimes sheets were glued or sewn together to make long rolls of paper, usually about thirty feet long, although one roll has been discovered that is 130 feet. Each end of the roll was attached to a handle to make winding easier. Even the brushes used for writing on this paper came from the papyrus, made from the thin stalks of the plume.

Paper made from this reed has given us some of the earliest records of the ancient civilizations of the eastern Mediterranean, stories of great events as well as glimpses of everyday life—marriage records, business accounts, and personal letters. The ancient Greeks obtained their supplies of paper from the port of Byblos, in what is now Lebanon. Their word for book—*biblion*—was derived from the name of this port, and in that way we obtained our English word "Bible" for the Book of Books.

Sacred ibis, papyrus, crocodile

The Hyksos who had been friendly to the descendants of Joseph and his brothers, were driven from Egypt 3,550 years ago, and Egyptian pharaohs ruled again. They were unfriendly to the Hebrews, and about 3,250 years ago the pharaoh ordered all Hebrew male infants to be killed. Only one escaped this terrible edict. He was hidden in a basket made of woven bulrushes, and the basket was floated among the reeds that grew along the edge of the Nile. When Pharaoh's daughter came to the river to bathe, she found the infant, adopted him, and brought him up in the royal palace. She gave him the Egyptian name Moses, which meant simply "child."

The young Moses was probably educated in the Egyptian sciences and arts. He no doubt learned to read and write Egyptian hieroglyphics. Hieroglyphics—derived from two Greek words that mean "sacred carvings," since the signs were chiseled on stone at first—were the basic writing system in Egypt at the time of Moses. Egyptian writing originated in the drawing of pictures of objects, such as a snake, a lion, a clump of papyrus, or perhaps an eye. About 750 pictures were used which at first meant only the things being pictured. There were, for example, at least twenty-two signs for various birds, such as the curved neck of the Egyptian vulture, the flat face of an owl, the tail feathers of the pintail duck.

Animal symbols used as hieroglyphs

Later the hieroglyphics came to represent ideas associated with the objects. A picture of a bull might also mean strength. Even so, hieroglyphic writing was limited, and ideas of even slight complexity were inexpressible. A further advance came when a picture represented not the object or the idea, but rather the first syllable of the name for the object. For example, a picture of a house stood for the Egyptian word *beth*, and therefore it represented the syllable "be."

A few hundred years after the time of Moses, the Phoenicians in the Holy Land invented the alphabet as we know it. They simply took the Egyptian syllabic signs and used each to represent a single sound. In this way the picture of a house became the second letter of the alphabet, B, in Phoenician—and in Hebrew also, for the Hebrews derived their alphabet from the Phoenicians. The Phoenicians and the Hebrews used only twenty-two symbols, that is, letters, and they had no letters for the vowels. The alphabet quickly spread throughout the Mediterranean world colonized by the Phoenicians. About 800 B.C. it was transmitted to the Greeks, who improved on it by adding vowels. This is the alphabet that spread to the Romans, who passed it on to us in almost its present form.

Although Moses was reared as an Egyptian, he did not forget his loyalty to his own people. One day he watched the Hebrews laboring for their Egyptian masters and saw an overseer beat a worker. Egyptian texts confirm that about that time Habiru were engaged in dragging stones for temples built by Pharaoh Ramses II. Moses killed the overseer and fled into the desert wastes of the Sinai Peninsula. There he saw a bush that "burned with fire, and the bush was not consumed" (Exodus 3:2). This bush may have been a thorny acacia, and the flame that seemed to leap out of it may have been a crimson mistletoe that grows as a parasite only upon this plant. When in bloom, the flame-colored flowers of the mistletoe make the shrub seem to blaze.

Moses returned to Egypt and began the long struggle with Pharaoh to liberate his people. Plague after plague struck the Egyptians. The first nine plagues were all natural disasters that have always occurred at one time or another in the Nile Valley, but probably never before had they occurred with such violence or so close together.

The first plague was the turning of the waters of the Nile to the color of blood. Such discoloration may have been due to reddish soils carried downstream by the floodwaters of the Nile. Or the cause may have been an abundance in the water of microorganisms containing a reddish pigment. Study of "red plagues" around the world in recent years has shown that certain water-inhabiting microorganisms are capable of phenomenal increases in numbers in a very short time. During one outbreak in Florida, for example, their numbers soared from only a few to six thousand in a single drop of water in a mere several days. And they released into the water a deadly toxin that caused the death of so many millions of fish that the shores stank and no one could go near the poisoned waters. The same thing seems to have happened in Egypt, for Exodus relates (7:21) that "the fish that was in the river died; and the river stank, and the Egyptians could not drink of the water of the river."

The second plague occurred when "frogs came up, and covered the land of Egypt" (Exodus 8:6). Frogs and toads are amphibians, a word derived from the Greek that means "living two lives." The first part of their life cycle after hatching, usually called the tadpole stage, must be spent in water. Only after a frog or a toad changes to an adult— that is, grows limbs, loses its tail, and develops lungs instead of gills—can it live on dry land.

The eggs of amphibians in desert areas usually hatch only during the seasons when there is sufficient moisture for the tadpoles to survive. Sometimes, though, an exceptionally heavy rainstorm or a sudden flash flood, both common in deserts, may cause the eggs to hatch at the wrong time of the year. This moisture may be sufficient to permit hatching, but not sufficient to enable the frogs to complete their life cycle and reach maturity. If this is indeed what occurred in Egypt, then millions of frogs must have perished all at once when they were left without water. Their bodies must have decayed in the blazing sun, and the Bible does state that the Egyptians "gathered them together upon heaps" (Exodus 8:14).

The third plague—the rising of "lice" and their attacks on man and beast—can also be explained as the result of the same out-of-season rainstorm or flood. The word translated as "lice" probably referred to the mosquito, the female of which feeds on the blood of man and animals. We often associate mosquitoes with damp woodlands, but they also occur in deserts where they are adapted to the dry conditions. Some kinds of mosquitoes lay their eggs in dry places which later become filled with water during the rainy or flood seasons. Then the tiny larvae hatch out, feed in the water, and, before the pools dry up, quickly transform into winged adults. Some kinds of desert mosquitoes can pass through the entire life cycle from egg to winged adult in a mere ten days.

The fourth plague was the swarm of flies, and they probably fed on the decaying bodies of frogs which littered the land. The fifth plague—a murrain, or disease, of domestic animals—was a natural outcome of the plague of flies. Numerous kinds of flies in addition to the common housefly exist, and many of them are extremely harmful to domestic animals. Screwworm flies lay their eggs in the skin of cattle, botflies attack the breathing passages of sheep, tsetse flies cause the n'gana disease of cattle as well as sleeping sickness in humans. And the sixth plague—boils —might have resulted from the attacks of the flies that laid their eggs in the skin of the Egyptians.

The seventh plague—the rain of hail—is another natural phenomenon that occurs throughout the deserts of the world, although one may not expect to find stones of ice in hot climates. Hailstorms, however, are not at all unusual in Egypt and the Holy Land. They were an ever-present threat to the ancient farmers, and Isaiah spoke (28:2) of the "tempest of hail" that beats down the grain before it can be harvested.

Hail is formed in much the same way as sleet, but a slight difference accounts for the larger size of the hailstones. When rain falls from a layer of warm air, and then passes through a layer of cold air before reaching the earth, the result is not snow but the little ice pellets called sleet. The more time the ice pellets spend aloft in the cold air, the more layers of snow and ice they accumulate around their central core. If the icy particles descend fairly rapidly through the layer of cold air, the hailstones may be as small as a pea. But if they are tossed about for a long time in the cold layer they may reach the size of golf balls. In the description of this seventh plague, the Bible refers to "fire mingled with the hail" (Exodus 9:24). This is indeed a precise observation of the lightning that usually accompanies the storms through which hailstones pass on their fall to earth.

Even after the hailstones destroyed the crops of the

Egyptians, Pharaoh still did not carry out his promise to let the Israelites go. There then followed a plague of locusts that "covered the face of the whole earth, so that the land was darkened; and they did eat every herb of the land, and all the fruit of the trees which the hail had left: and there remained not any green thing" (Exodus 10:15). Such a picture of desolation due to locust hordes is no exaggeration. In recent years one black cloud of these insects, which entirely blotted out the sun, was estimated to have been a mile wide and more than fifty miles deep.

Locust is the name given to several kinds of grasshoppers that increase in numbers suddenly and then undertake mass migrations. It was not known until several decades ago that the solitary locust, which causes only minor damage, and the destructive swarming locust, which flies in clouds numbering in the billions, are actually the same insect. And it was only a few years ago that the complicated puzzle as to why a solitary locust sometimes turns into a swarming locust was at least partially solved.

Scientists learned that first there has to be a season of favorable weather and of abundant food, which causes the solitary locusts to increase greatly in numbers. Then there must follow a very unfavorable season for the locusts, which makes them crowd together on the sparse vegetation that survives. Crowding brings about chemical changes in the body of the female: more of her eggs hatch, and they do so in only about half the time normally required. The already-large number of locusts is now augmented by those that have hatched from the quickly developing eggs. Soon a cloud of locusts is aswarm over the land, darkening the sky and devouring any vegetation in sight.

The last of the nine natural plagues was the thick darkness over the land of Egypt, "even darkness which may be felt" (Exodus 10:21). One might at first think that this darkness was an eclipse, but the Bible specifically states that it lasted for three days and that it could be felt. It undoubtedly was a combination of dust storm, which blots out the sun for days, and sandstorm, which feels like the jabs of thousands of pins into the skin. Most people think that dust storms and sandstorms are the same, but they are not. Dust is light in weight, and a strong desert wind can lift clouds of these particles thousands of feet into the sky, causing darkness even at noontime. Sand, however, is much heavier and the wind cannot lift it very high. Instead, the sand is blown as a low, thick carpet that covers the surface of the ground. Since the sand particles are heavy, this carpet of churning sand is never more than a few feet high. That is why during a sandstorm the head and shoulders of a person appear to float in clear air, while the rest of his body is obscured by the grains, much as if he were wading waist-deep in water.

The first nine plagues were natural events familiar to anyone who lived in the deserts of the Near East or Africa. They can all be explained in modern scientific terms. But Pharaoh could not explain away the tenth, and most terrible, plague as a natural event. The firstborn of every living thing in Egypt—the child of Pharaoh himself, as well as the offspring of the beasts of the field—suddenly died, except for the Israelite children. The Israelites had been instructed by Moses to keep death from their houses by preparing a feast of lamb and sprinkling some of the lamb's blood on the doorposts so that death would "pass over" their houses. The Feast of Passover continues to be celebrated by Jews to this day, a constant reminder of the liberation from bondage. Jesus's Last Supper taken with his disciples was in reality the Passover Feast (Matthew 26:18).

Pharaoh could no longer attribute these plagues to natural calamities alone. He summoned Moses and agreed to his demand to let the Israelites leave Egypt and begin their long and arduous migration to Canaan.

V. Life in the Wilderness

Pharaoh regretted his decision to let the Israelites depart for the Promised Land, and he sent his charioteers in pursuit. The waters of a sea parted, allowing the Israelites through but not the pursuing Egyptians, who were engulfed. The King James Version states that the sea was the Red Sea, but scholars now know that this is a mistranslation of the Hebrew texts which state that it was "the Sea of Reeds." The Sea of Reeds was one of the countless shallow ponds, bordered with papyrus, between the Mediterranean Sea and the Gulf of Suez. The Suez Canal was cut through this marshy land in 1869, but several ponds still remain in that area. They ordinarily can be crossed with no more inconvenience than wet feet, but they become covered with water when there is a strong wind. Such a wind could have caused a surge in the waters, sweeping away the Egyptian soldiers, although the Israelites had been able to slosh through the mire only a short time before.

The Israelites had escaped from Pharaoh's army, but as they entered the wilderness of the Sinai Peninsula, they found that the supply of food they had carried out of Egypt was being used up quickly. They recalled the fruits and vegetables they had left behind, among them cucumbers which were widely cultivated in the rich mud along the Nile—the same cucumber as ours today, although somewhat smaller. Looking about them, the Israelites despaired of finding enough food for their great numbers in this desolate land. Then occurred in rapid succession two wondrous events: the descent of the quails, and the manna from heaven.

Exodus states (16:13) that in the evening "the quails came up, and covered the camp." The Israelites were undoubtedly familiar with quails, for wall paintings in Egyptian tombs dating from the time of the exodus show that people caught the birds in nets for food. Probably never before, though, had the Israelites seen so many of them at one time. The quail they saw is the only migratory quail in the world. It is a mottled brown and considerably smaller than the North American bobwhite quail. There are several kinds of North American quail, but none of them migrates from place to place across the land as the migratory quail of the Old World do. Instead, the seasonal movements of North American quail are vertical—down from the mountains to the protected valleys in autumn, then up to the higher slopes again the following spring.

Migratory quail are widespread across Europe, Asia, and much of Africa, but they never occurred in the New World until some were intentionally introduced in the last century. Thousands of them were imported one year in the hopes that they would become residents of North America also. The quail made nests, laid eggs, reared their young, and then in the autumn they took flight on a southward migration. They never returned. The birds had attempted to follow their ancestral migration route to the southeast, unaware that they were on a different continent. They perished over the vast stretches of the Atlantic Ocean and the Gulf of Mexico, except for the exhausted few that alighted on the decks of ships at sea.

Each spring and autumn quail still take wing on their migrations between the Sudan in Africa and western Asia and Europe, passing over the Sinai Peninsula and the Holy Land. Until this century, great clouds of them migrated in numbers probably approximating those of biblical times. Then they were decimated. In the early decades of this century Egyptians killed them by the millions for their feathers and for food. The rate of killing reached three million birds a year, and by the 1930s the huge flocks were largely gone. No one nowadays sees the spectacular numbers described in the Bible.

Migratory quail are short-winged and have only weak powers of flight. They are often blown off course by a strong wind and they fall exhausted onto the nearest land. This is indeed what must have happened when the quail descended on the Israelite camp, for the Bible states that there was a wind that brought forth the quail from the sea. The Bible also says that the quail fell to earth in the evening. That, too, accords well with what we know of the natural history of these birds, for the migratory quail usually flies at night.

The next morning "behold, upon the face of the wilderness there lay a small round thing, as small as the hoar frost on the ground. And when the children of Israel saw it, they said to one another, It is manna: for they wist not what it was. And Moses said unto them, This is the bread which the Lord hath given you to eat" (Exodus 16:14-15). Two words in this passage must be explained. "Manna" is a Hebrew word that does not refer to anything in particular, but simply means "What is it?" Also, the word translated as "bread" should more accurately have been translated as "food."

There has been considerable disagreement among Bible scholars as to exactly what manna signified. Some have thought it to be a lowly plant like an alga or a lichen, others that it was the gum from some tree. Most scholars now agree that manna is a substance produced by little insects which gorge themselves on the tamarisk shrubs that grow in the wetter parts of Sinai and the Holy Land. An abundance of scale insects, related to the common aphids and mealybugs, are often found sucking on the tender twigs of these shrubs. They puncture the twigs and sip up great quantities of the sap, but they use only a small part of it for themselves. Much of the sugar contained in the sap passes through their bodies and falls as droplets of sweet liquid, often called "honeydew," onto the leaves and ground. The rapid evaporation of moisture from this liquid, due to the dryness of the desert air, quickly solidifies the droplets into tiny flakes that the Bible describes as resembling hoarfrost.

The Israelites continued to head south across the Sinai Peninsula. At first the land was an almost featureless wil-

derness, relieved only by eroded hills and the dry beds of
rivers that had cut deeply into the land during the flood
seasons. Constantly before their eyes to the south was a
line of great mountains which, as they drew closer,
showed wild yellow, red, and purple hues. Within three
months after their escape from Egypt, the Israelites had
reached the foot of Mount Sinai, a solid block of reddish
granite that rises steeply out of the desert. Its height is
about three thousand feet, not much in comparison with
most mountains, but it looms so dramatically out of the
surrounding land that the Israelites must have thought it
a fitting place for God to dwell.

Several times Moses climbed the barren eroded slopes
to the summit, and it was there that he heard the words:
"Ye have seen what I did unto the Egyptians, and how I
bare you on eagles' wings, and brought you unto myself"
(Exodus 19:4). Weary of the searing wilderness through
which they traveled, the Israelites must have received
great encouragement when they saw the eagles wheeling
so effortlessly in the sky. The eagle, among the most majestic of birds, has often been the symbol of confidence and
power. The United States of America carries the eagle on
its Great Seal, and in the ancient world it was the emblem
of the Assyrian, Babylonian, Persian, Roman, and other
empires.

In most passages in the Bible the eagle referred to is the
golden eagle, which inhabits Africa, Asia, and Europe, as
well as North America. The Palestinian form of this bird
is dark brown in color, the back of its neck sprinkled with
gold. The wingspread of a large specimen may reach
nearly eight feet. It is primarily a bird of the mountains,

where it builds huge nests of sticks piled on rocky crags. But it may often be seen far from the mountains, patrolling at low altitudes in its search for prey. It usually feeds on small mammals, such as hares and rodents, and its attacks on livestock have been greatly exaggerated.

An eagle stays aloft for hours, only occasionally beating its immense wings. It is not defying the laws of gravity; it simply seems to be. Gravity is constantly at work pulling the bird downward, but another force is keeping it aloft. This force is the rising currents of air which are produced in several ways. Wind may strike a mountain ridge, be deflected, and rise upward. An even greater flow of air, known as a thermal, is due to the unequal heating of the earth's surface by the sun. The broad outspread wings of the eagle take advantage of the lift produced by upcurrents and thermals. Even though the wings of an eagle seem motionless, they do move slightly. They change direction to keep the bird on top of the upward current, producing the well-known spiraling flight.

After a few years in the wilderness, Moses approached the borders of the Promised Land. He sent out scouts to reconnoiter. The scouts reported that the people in Canaan are "of a great stature . . . giants" (Numbers 13:32-33). The giants were probably tall burial stones, known as dolmens, which the Canaanites placed over graves. Archaeologists have discovered dolmens near the very places where the scouts reported seeing them.

The scouts were frightened and they returned to the camp bearing clusters of grapes and pomegranates as proof that they had at least entered the land of Canaan. "Pomegranate" means literally "apple with grains," and that is a fitting description of the fruit, for it contains many red-colored seeds surrounded by juicy pulp. The pomegranate grows wild as a large shrub or a small tree in many parts of the Near East. Since biblical times it has been valued by travelers in this thirsty land for its fruit full of juice. So important was the pomegranate in the life of the Israelites that it was used as a design to decorate the Temple and on coins issued in Jerusalem.

Pomegranate

Moses was so angered by the fear of the scouts that he led the tribes southward again into Sinai for further toughening by the desert. During their years in the wilderness, the Israelites celebrated the liberation from Egypt with a Passover feast of "unleavened bread and bitter herbs" (Numbers 9:11). Unleavened bread is a flat cake of ground wheat flour made without yeast. This flat bread recalled to the Israelites their hurried exodus from Egypt when there was not time to bring with them yeast to make the dough rise. Yeast is related to mushrooms, toadstools, and molds, but it has several unique characteristics of its own. These other fungi grow by putting out thin, many-celled strands, but yeast consists of only a single exceedingly small cell, about three-thousandths of an inch long. Nor does yeast grow the fruiting bodies known as mushrooms or toadstools; it reproduces by simple cell division.

The most distinctive thing about yeast is that it can utilize its food in the absence of oxygen. It can live under conditions that would suffocate almost all other kinds of plants and animals. And in the process of utilizing its food, it brings about a chemical reaction which changes sugar into alcohol and carbon dioxide. Carbon dioxide gas is what does the work in making bread "rise." The yeast that today's housewife buys for baking is really yeast cells mixed with starch, and then compacted into small squares. In biblical times, a bit of the dough was reserved before baking and kept to leaven the next batch.

The bitter herbs mentioned in the biblical story may have included chicory, wild lettuce, and several other plants whose leaves were gathered for use in salads, but they were most probably dandelions. Nowadays dandelion is a common weed that plagues the lawns of homeowners in many other parts of the world, but its original home was in the lands bordering the Mediterranean. You often see its featherlike seeds flying through the air, and on a windy day there may be so many of them they look like snow-flakes. These seeds have become lodged in man's belong-ings and trade items, and in that way accidentally have been spread around the world.

The Israelites traveled through a "great and terrible wil-derness, wherein were fiery serpents, and scorpions" (Deu-teronomy 8:15). These two creatures—the serpent with poison in its fangs, and the scorpion with poison at the tip of its abdomen—were often used in the Bible to express danger or desolation. To the ancients the scorpion was one of the most fearsome of animals, nearly, in spite of its small size, as much so as the lion. Its abdomen tapers to a long curving "tail" which is held over the body and ends in a poison-injecting sting. The sting can give a painful, and sometimes deadly, dose of poison, although the deadliness of most scorpions has been much overrated. The really large species of scorpions, about ten inches in length, are comparatively harmless to humans, but the stings of several small-sized ones may be fatal.

Scorpions are creatures of the night, hiding in crevices and under rocks during the day. When a scorpion finds a large insect or a spider, it grasps it with its mouthparts, which are large and resemble lobster claws, and then pro-ceeds to tear it to bits. The sting is used only when the prey is large enough to offer resistance, or when the scor-pion is threatened by an enemy. Scorpions are always solitary except at mating time, and even then the female may resort to cannibalism, devouring the male with whom she has just mated. The hostility of scorpions to their own kind must have seemed particularly loathsome to the Israelites, who depended upon cooperation for survival in the desert.

The serpents are not named according to species in the Bible, but two highly poisonous kinds probably were meant: the horned viper and the asp. The horned viper, which lives in the deserts of Egypt and Arabia, is excellently adapted to life in the sands. It is almost the same color as sand, it can bury itself quickly, and it moves through the shifting grains by a sidewinding motion (similar to that of the sidewinder rattlesnake of the United States Southwest, to which it is not closely related). The horned viper possesses sawlike scales along the sides of its body which allow it to sink vertically into the sand. When it moves its body from side to side, these scales work the grains from underneath its body onto its back. The closely-related false horned viper is even better adapted to desert life. Not only can it bury itself, but it also possesses a valvelike structure inside its nostrils and an especially tight closure of the lips, both defenses against wind-driven sand.

The asp is a cobra, and it is thought to have been the snake that killed Cleopatra when Egypt was about to fall to the Roman armies. Like the Indian cobra used by snake charmers, the ribs of the neck spread out to form a wide hood, which is used to threaten enemies. The Egyptian cobra does not have so large a hood as the Indian one, but its bite is no less deadly. The asp was sacred to the Egyptians and the headdress on the figures in many Egyptian sculptures represents the hood of this cobra.

Finally the desert-toughened Israelites were poised on the eastern frontiers of Canaan, a land "flowing with milk and honey" (Exodus 3:8). Milk and honey were the two products most commonly associated with Canaan. By the time of Moses domesticated cattle had become abundant in Canaan, where they fed on the rich grasses that grew after the winter rainy season. Honey, an important sweetener, was collected from wild bees and it was traded widely by desert nomads.

Moses called the Israelites together at the base of Mount Pisgah, which means "split mountain," so named because of its shape. There he delivered the three great orations that make up the book of Deuteronomy (Greek for "second law," that is, the law after the Ten Commandments).

The biblical laws about the treatment and protection of animals are humane. The Ten Commandments themselves

Egyptian cobra

decree a Sabbath or day of rest for animals as well as for man, and elsewhere in the Bible there are constant references to the kindness with which animals must be treated. Anyone seeing an animal too heavily burdened must stop to help unload it, even though the animal might belong to an enemy. It was forbidden to remove a bird from its eggs or to muzzle an ox when it was at work threshing grain. Hunting as a sport was not approved of. Esau's fondness for hunting was condemned in the Bible, for he is described as being "a cunning hunter." His brother Jacob, in contrast, was lauded as "a plain man" (Genesis 25:27) who dwelt in a tent and kept flocks and herds.

The laws of Moses about the kinds of animals that might or might not be eaten reveal some of the animals with which the Israelites were most familiar. The only kind of animal that could serve for food was one that "parteth the hoof, and is clovenfooted, and cheweth the cud" (Leviticus 11:3). This sentence automatically eliminated the camel and the lion and other mammals without hoofs, the horse which is not clovenfooted, and swine which do not chew their cud. The word "clovenfooted" is often not understood by readers of the Bible. Zoologists divide the hoofed mammals—that is, those with at least some of their toes enclosed inside a covering of horn—into two general groups. One group has an odd number of toes on each foot, and the other an even number. The horse was the only odd-toed hoofed mammal inhabiting the ancient Near East. It stands on a single toe, which we usually call the hoof. The even-toed hoofed mammals are the ones called in the Bible "clovenfooted," although the cleft is really only a slight gap between the toes of the hoof. Clovenfooted mammals are a very diverse group that includes sheep, goats, cows, swine, camels, hippopotami, deer, and antelopes—but only those clovenfooted mammals that chew the cud were acceptable.

Mammals particularly desirable as food were sheep, goats, cows, and also the "hart, and the roebuck, and the fallow deer, and the wild goat, and the pygarg, and the wild ox, and the chamois" (Deuteronomy 14:5). The hart is the male of an animal known in the Old World as the red deer, a very close relative of the North American elk or wapiti. (The female is called a hind.) It is an extraordinarily adaptable animal that is native from the cold heaths of Scotland to the dry plains of the Caucasus. Judging by the more than twenty mentions of harts and hinds in the Bible, it once must have been very common in the Holy Land.

The "roebuck" probably is a mistranslation. The English translators of the Bible thought that the Hebrew word for this mammal referred to the male of the roe deer, a forest animal common across northern Europe and Asia. The roebuck probably was not intended, but rather the gazelle, a graceful game animal of the Near East. Gazelles are medium-sized antelopes and are such fast runners that ingenious methods have been devised to hunt them. Sometimes they are panicked so that they will flee into a net or an enclosure. Falcons and greyhounds have been trained to attack them and slow them down until the hunters can catch up. And today they are hunted from small planes.

The fallow deer was most likely not meant either, since this deer does not range as far south as the deserts through which Moses traveled. Some scholars believe that the original Hebrew should have been translated instead as "hartebeest," an antelope that once was widespread in Egypt, Sinai, and parts of the Holy Land. The hartebeest is rare in the Holy Land now, although it is still prevalent in Africa. But in biblical times it must have been abundant, for the Bible states that it supplied vast quantities of meat for Solomon's feasts. The pygarg is another member of the antelope family, possibly the addax antelope of North Africa and western Asia. Its horns are among the most extraordinary worn by any animal: each is long, thin, and has a double twist.

The chamois represents yet another mistranslation, for chamois are native to the mountains of Europe and there is no evidence that they ever inhabited the Holy Land. The animal probably intended was the Barbary or wild sheep of North Africa. Its range once extended eastward to Sinai, but now it is virtually extinct east of the Nile River. The Barbary sheep is related to, and much resembles, the bighorn sheep of the western mountains of North America. Its horns are massive spirals about two feet in length. It has a coat of stiff hairs rather than the soft fleece of the barnyard animal, and it is much more agile.

The wild ox, or aurochs, was the ancestor of our domesticated cattle. It is also the animal that in most versions of the Bible has been mistranslated as "unicorn" (Numbers 24:8; Deuteronomy 33:17), the single-horned beast of Greek mythology. Aurochs bulls were quite large, and their horns were extremely long. The Hebrews made from these horns drinking vessels that had a capacity up to four gallons. While a general in Gaul, Caesar was impressed by the aurochs' size and power, although he exaggerated when he stated that it was almost as large as an elephant. The aurochs was widespread in Europe, North Africa, and the Near East in ancient times, but the last survivor died in Poland in 1627. We are fortunate, though, to know exactly what the aurochs looked like, for there are several clear illustrations and descriptions of it. It measured six and a half feet in height at the shoulder. The bull was black with a white or reddish stripe along its back and white curly hair between the horns. The cows were mostly brownish-red in color.

In 1921 it occurred to a German scientist that he might be able to "reconstruct" the extinct aurochs by scientifically cross-breeding many kinds of domestic cattle that still possessed its characteristics. After a very complicated series of crosses was made, the attempt was successful. The reconstructed aurochs look very much like their ancestors,

Aurochs

although of course they can never be exactly alike. They also act like the extinct animals: they are agile runners, unlike modern cattle, and they are also fierce and temperamental. Several dozen of them are now alive in zoos in Germany and Poland.

No one knows exactly when and where the aurochs was domesticated. Several Mesopotamian paintings and sculptures dating from about 4,500 years ago show domesticated breeds of cattle obviously derived from the aurochs, so domestication must have begun much earlier than that. Ancient Egypt, too, was familiar with this animal. One hunting scene carved on the temple of Ramses III shows this Pharaoh shooting with a bow and arrow from a chariot. One aurochs lies on its back dead and two others are dying from their wounds.

Moses died before the Israelites entered Canaan. He was succeeded as leader by Joshua, who struck westward across the Jordan River almost immediately. It was spring, and the waters of the Jordan should have been swollen by runoff from melting snows on the mountains. Yet the Israelites crossed on a dry riverbed. The Jordan Valley is in an earthquake zone, and landslides touched off by an earthquake upstream could have dammed the river. Such damming of the Jordan by landslides has occurred at least three times in this century.

Jericho, an imposing fortress near where the Jordan enters the Dead Sea, stood in the way of the Israelites, but with the blasts of the ram's horn, or *shofar*, the walls tumbled down. The *shofar* has been translated in the Bible as "horn," "cornet," or most often as "trumpet." The ancient breeds of sheep often bore huge horns from which musical instruments were made. The horn was heated with steam until it was soft enough for its natural curve to be straightened out. Then the wide end, where the horn had been attached to the ram, was bent at almost a right angle.

Archaeological excavations have been made at the mound that represents the ancient city of Jericho, about a mile or so northwest of the modern city. As the archaeologists dug downward they found not one ancient city but rather successive cities, each built atop the ruins of the previous ones. Jericho was discovered to be the earliest known town in the world, its settlement beginning about eleven thousand years ago. Above the first signs of human habitation, five cities were built in antiquity—and the fourth of these appears to be the one that was conquered by Joshua. The archaeologists discovered that it had been fortified by double walls nearly thirty feet high, each wall about six feet thick. It was clear to the excavators that this city had a violent end. Sections of the wall had crumbled due to an earthquake, and there was evidence of a fire so intense that it burned bricks and cracked stones.

To the Canaanites who built Jericho, these walls must have seemed impregnable. They were—to everything except earthquakes. Major earthquakes occur in the Jordan Valley on the average of once every twenty-five years, and minor tremors much more often than that. The last serious earthquake in the Holy Land was in 1927, but lesser ones have occurred since that were severe enough to damage buildings in Jerusalem. Earthquakes are frequently mentioned in the Bible, and they are sometimes regarded as natural disasters since "the Lord was not in the earthquake" (I Kings 19:11).

Such earthquakes are caused by pressures in the surface layers of the earth. The crust of the earth—with its mountains, valleys, sea basins, and other irregularities—is like a flagstone terrace in which the stones have been poorly laid. Such a crust can endure strains placed on it only to a limited extent. To compensate for the strain, there usually is a shift in a nearby weak portion of the crust. Earthquakes occur primarily in two zones. One sweeps around the borders of the Pacific Ocean, the other underlies the entire Mediterranean region, including the Holy Land, and extends as far as eastern Asia.

Archaeologists have unearthed other evidence that confirms the advance of the Israelites into the Promised Land. At least six cities west of the Jordan were discovered to have been destroyed approximately 3,200 years ago, when the invasion under Joshua was taking place. There is even a written record from Egypt dating from that time that tells of a pharaoh's dealings with "the people of Israel" in Canaan.

Canaan included most of the area traditionally known as the Holy Land west of the Jordan, but near the Sea of Galilee it extended a considerable distance eastward. Canaan means "land of purple" and it took its name from the purplish dye, extracted from a seashell, that was one of its principal exports. Canaanites probably originated slightly less than five thousand years ago as a Semitic people from Arabia or the lands around the Persian Gulf. Within only a thousand years after that they had reached the height of their power, but within a further few centuries they were overrun by Hittites, Egyptians, and Hyksos.

By the time that Joshua began his invasion, Canaan was divided into a number of small states like Jericho, each a

fortified city with its own king. Each city usually domi-
nated a caravan trade route through which the traffic
between Egypt and the Fertile Crescent flowed, and it is
believed that these cities exacted tolls from the caravans. The
rulers of Canaan lived in luxury inside the high walls of
their cities, but the common people were sunk in squalor,
clustered in small settlements of mud houses. They were
serfs, toiling while the ruling class amused itself with imi-
tations of Egyptian art, music, and literature. The country's
glory had faded, its vigor sapped by the luxurious living
of the kings and wasted by wars. Canaan became a
mere vassal of Egypt, to which the local kings had to pay
tribute and to provide laborers for building irrigation works
and temples. The Israelites overran most of Canaan at the
same time that the Philistines, sometimes called the "Sea
People," invaded the coast. The Canaanites retreated
northward into the Lebanon Mountains and a narrow strip
of coast that later came to be known as Phoenicia.

Canaanites and Phoenicians worshiped many nature
gods. Chief among them was Baal who was regarded as
master of the earth, his arm hurling bolts of lightning and
his voice causing thunder. The Israelites referred to Baal
as Baal-zebul or Beelzebub, which means "lord of the flies,"
a name that no doubt referred to the hordes of flies that
buzzed around the animals sacrificed to this god. By New
Testament times Beelzebub had become a title for Satan.
A Mother Goddess also was worshiped in a place the Bible refers to as "a grove." This may have been a tree
planted by the Canaanites, but more usually it was a
wooden pole, held in place in a stone base, that was probably carved to represent the tree of life.

The Israelites conquered Canaan with the speed of a

Shittah tree (acacia)

whirlwind. The Twelve Tribes then drew lots for their choice of land. Joshua was assigned a town of his own in the central highlands of Ephraim, north of Jerusalem. In ancient times Ephraim was blessed "for the precious fruits brought forth by the sun" (Deuteronomy 33:14). It is still very productive, everywhere dotted with orchards and with nearly continuous groves of olives. Joshua ordered the Israelites to construct their first city in the Promised Land: Shiloh (now known as Seilun).

He brought to Shiloh the sacred Ark of the Covenant, which was placed in a tentlike Tabernacle. The Ark was a huge chest that contained the stone tablets of the Ten Commandments. Its wood was obtained from the "shittah" tree, which most scholars now agree meant the acacia, a thorny but sweet-smelling tree that abounds in the Bible lands. The outside bark of the acacia is gnarled and dark, and you would not suspect that the wood underneath has a beautiful orange grain. It also has the advantage of being resistant to the attacks of most insects.

Above the chest hovered the wings of two cherubim. Today a cherub is pictured as a winged child, but this is an incorrect impression obtained from the paintings of Italian artists of some five hundred years ago. Actually, by the time of Jesus, people had forgotten what cherubim signified, and the historian Josephus wrote in the first century A.D. that "no one can tell what they were like." But now archaeology has unearthed much of the forgotten past of the biblical world, and it is believed that a cherub was a small wing-bearing lion with a human head, in other words, a sphinx. Excavations have revealed that this was the winged creature most often portrayed in Canaanite art, and Canaanite kings are often shown seated on thrones supported by two cherubim. The Israelites probably adapted the cherubim to make a throne for the invisible presence of God.

The tent of the Tabernacle was covered by badger skins. Such skins are mentioned several times in the Old Testament, and it is apparent that they were highly valued, for they are usually listed along with gold, jewels, and other precious objects. Most badger pelts are extremely durable and tough, adapted to the rough work of digging in the ground. They must have made excellent weatherproofing for the Tabernacle. The Near Eastern badger is short-legged and its burly body appears to crawl on the ground. The front feet are armed with powerful claws that can

Cherub

move a great amount of earth in a short time, useful both in digging its own burrow and also in digging out animals it preys upon. The particular species of badger mentioned in the Bible may have been the honey badger, which ranges from Africa to India. Honey badgers in particular have a thick loose skin. In fact, the skin is like an oversized coat. If this animal is grasped behind the neck, it can twist about inside its skin to bite the hand that holds it.

After dividing up Canaan, the Israelites instituted a more democratic way of life than had ever existed there before. They felt that one King in heaven was enough, and for many generations they were ruled only by Judges. The Judges were not judges as we use the term today, but rather particularly forceful leaders who were elected to command in times of trouble. The rule by the Judges was possibly the world's earliest experiment in democracy. As the Israelites settled down in the land of Canaan their population grew rapidly. To provide food, the forests were rapidly cleared and herds of sheep, goats, and cows increased. Agriculture assumed more importance than animal husbandry: orchards of fruit and nut trees were planted, and gardens were laid out. Much of the wilderness of the Holy Land was tamed, and it was a period of great changes in the face of the land.

VI. Nature Wisdom of David and Solomon

A constant threat to the Twelve Tribes was posed by the Philistines, known in Egyptian records as the "Sea People." They descended on the Holy Land from the islands of the Aegean Sea, between Greece and Turkey, plundering the cities of Asia Minor along the way. Their stronghold was the coastal plain, along which they established five cities mentioned in the Bible: Gaza, Gath, Ashdod, Ekron, and Ashkelon. Ashkelon in particular was famed in the ancient world for the profusion of fruits and vegetables that grew in its fertile soil. One vegetable was the small onion or scallion, for which the city became noted in Roman times. In fact, our word "scallion" comes from the Latin *caepa Ascalonia*, which means "onion of Ashkelon."

The Philistines held a monopoly on the manufacture of iron and in this way exerted control over the Israelites. Iron was far superior to the bronze used for weapons by the Israelites. It was stronger, and it was also more easily obtainable, making a large number of weapons available for the Philistines. Bronze was often in·short supply because tin, combined with copper to make this alloy, was rare. Iron, on the other hand, was very abundant, and learning how to smelt it caused an armaments revolution. The Philistines jealously guarded the secrets of the complicated smelting process, and they prevented the Israelites from stocking up on iron swords and shields by not allowing them to have smiths in their territory. Only after the first kings of Israel, Saul and David, defeated the Philistines did the metal come into common use. The Israelites quickly learned the techniques of iron-making from the Philistines and even the Hebrew words for "knife" and "helmet" came from them.

The youthful shepherd David slew the Philistine giant Goliath with a stone hurled from his sling. David had acquired his skill while fighting off wild animals, such as bears, which attempted to prey on his flocks. The bear is mentioned often in the Bible, and it was regarded as second in fierceness only to the lion. Bears apparently once were extremely abundant in the Holy Land. The clearing of their forest habitat and the deadliness of the modern gun have virtually eliminated them from the Near East, except for a few that survive in remote parts of Syria and Lebanon.

David was a remarkable leader who defeated all of Israel's enemies and ushered in a Golden Age that began about three thousand years ago. Among David's victories was the conquest of the city of Jebus, whose name he changed to Jerusalem, which means "City of Peace." Jerusalem is situated on a limestone ridge about 2,500 feet above sea level. To the south and west is the valley of Hinnom (or Gehenna) which was used to burn refuse. By New Testament times Gehenna had become a symbol for Hell, probably because of the fires constantly burning there. To the east was Jerusalem's main supply of water, the spring of Gihon, which means "the gusher." The spring got its name because it does not produce water in a steady flow, but rather collects it in an underground reservoir from which it suddenly gushes out when full. The Jebusites had cut a long narrow shaft through the rocks to connect the city with the water supply so they could reach it in time of siege. David took the city by surprise by entering it through this secret shaft (as told in II Samuel 5:8).

David was more than a great warrior. He was a musician who played the eight-stringed harplike instrument known as the lyre and a great poet who composed about half of the Psalms. The Psalms employ a rich use of natural history in their vivid images, and they reveal a keen awareness of the links between man and nature.

In Psalm 55 David laments: "Oh that I had wings like a dove! for then would I fly away, and be at rest." David, weighed down by the duties of statecraft, must often have wished he could take flight from his tasks. He might have selected almost any bird to express this wish, yet he chose the dove for a particular reason. This knowledgeable former shepherd knew that while most birds can fly, only doves can take off with a sudden burst of speed and sustain their powerful flight for a long distance.

The habits of the Palestinian house sparrow were so well known that Psalm 102 uses it as a symbol of desolation: "I

watch, and am as a sparrow alone upon the house top."
Here is an intentional contradiction, for it is difficult to visualize a lone sparrow. House sparrows are highly gregarious
birds, seeking food in large flocks and at night assembling
in protected places, such as under the roof eaves of buildings. Thus, this Psalm's unlikely picture of a single sparrow evokes a feeling of utter loneliness and abandonment.
This house sparrow, by the way, is closely related to the
English sparrow, which was introduced into North America
in 1852 and has now spread to all populated parts of
the continent.

In the same Psalm occurs the line: "I am like a pelican
of the wilderness." The white pelican is abundant around
the inland lakes and rivers of Africa and Eurasia where it
preys on fish. Its Hebrew name means "the disgorger,"
which it received because it stores captured fish in a pouch
under its bill and then disgorges them to feed its young.
Many Bible readers have wondered what the water-inhabiting pelican was doing in the wilderness. In the Bible the
word "wilderness" referred to any unpopulated place, such
as a mountain or a desert or a marsh. Pelicans are often
found living in the deserts of the Bible lands, so long as
there is an inland lake within flying distance.

In addition to the numerous descriptions of birds in the
Psalms, many poetic images make use of plants. David's
Psalm 37 contains a line frequently quoted: "I have seen
the wicked in great power, and spreading himself like a
green bay tree." David could have selected no better tree
as a symbol of overreaching power. Numerous shoots
sprout from the ground near its main stem, and that is why
this tree appears to be "spreading." The evergreen luxuri-

ance of the bay tree's leaves symbolized to David the prosperity enjoyed by the wicked. Later, in the time of the Greeks and Romans, this tree was known as the laurel and its leaves were awarded to victors in the Olympic Games and to heroes returning from war.

Another noted tree of the Psalms is the weeping willow: "By the rivers of Babylon, there we sat down, yea, we wept . . . We hanged our harps upon the willows in the midst thereof" (Psalm 137:1-2). A legend grew that the lyres so weighted down the branches that they drooped as if weeping ever afterward. When the weeping willow was widely planted in European gardens, and later in those of North America, the legend followed the tree. It is now known, however, that the weeping willow is native to China, and it most probably had not been introduced into the Near East at the time this Psalm was written. Some other tree must have been meant by the Hebrew word translated as willow. It was probably the aspen. Because of an unusual way in which the stalks of the leaves are attached to the branches, the leaves droop as if weeping.

David's son Solomon, in the fourth year of his reign, began work on the magnificent Temple at Jerusalem. The walls of the Temple were built of marble, but they were roofed and lined inside with wood from the cedar of Lebanon. This tree, the largest and most noble growing in the Bible lands, once was abundant in what are now Lebanon, Syria, and Turkey. It towered as high as 120 feet, and the diameter of its trunk sometimes reached eight feet. It exuded a fragrant gum that made walking in a cedar grove a delight to the sense of smell as well as to the sense of

Cedar of Lebanon

sight. Its wood not only was a beautiful reddish color, but it also resisted decay and attack by insects.

There was commerce in its logs long before the time of Solomon. About 4,700 years ago, in the reign of Snefu of Egypt, the details of a business transaction on the Lebanese coast were scratched on a tablet: "We brought forty ships laden with cedar trunks . . . We made the doors of the king's palace of cedar wood." Solomon had the big trees felled by the thousands to supply timber for the Temple and for his fabulous palace, which he named "The House of the Forest of Lebanon." He sent shifts of ten thousand Israelites a month to aid the native workers in devastating these forests.

Today the hills that once were clothed with cedars are barren slopes. Fortunately some scattered groves survived the axes of empire after empire that attacked them. One such grove, now pitifully small, is preserved in a park about eighty miles north of Beirut, Lebanon. The entire grove contains only a few hundred cedars in a place where once were tens of thousands. A few even smaller groves are scattered throughout Lebanon, including one on Mount Lebanon which has been protected by a monastery. Nowadays all cedars growing anywhere in Lebanon are rigidly protected against cutting. Efforts have been made to replant cedars in other places in Lebanon, but it is a slow and difficult task. And to bring back whole forests of them to their ancient splendor would be a planting job to awe even a Johnny Appleseed. However, the cedar of Lebanon is now prospering far from its home. Seeds have been sent around the world and they have taken root in many places in Europe and North America.

Forest trees served as a symbol of holiness to the Israelites. The names of both the oak and the terebinth, the two most common forest trees of the Holy Land, were derived from Hebrew words meaning "God." Most of the valleys are too hot for oaks, but five kinds are found on the cooler mountainsides. About nine-tenths of the trees growing on Mount Carmel, for example, are kermes oaks. The terebinth is a large tree with straggling branches that much resembles an oak in shape and in bark. It is common on the lower slopes of hills in localities too hot or too dry for oaks. Its trunk yields a fragrant resinous juice, and it is probably for this reason that it also has been called the "turpentine tree."

Among other timbers Solomon imported from Lebanon was the Grecian juniper (the tree that was probably meant by the word "algum" in the Bible). It was the only tree of the Holy Land that rivaled the cedar of Lebanon in size and beauty, and it is still common in mountain woods in Lebanon, Syria, and parts of northern Israel. The "fir" tree (I Kings 5:8, 10, and elsewhere) was actually a pine, probably the Aleppo pine, which grows to a height of sixty feet and is abundant on dry hills. The "chestnut tree" (Ezekiel 31:8, and elsewhere) is not the tree that we know as the chestnut, but rather the plane tree, which was widespread near rivers. The hardy and attractive plane has been introduced around the world and it is today one of the trees often planted along city streets.

Before he died, David made a conquest in the Negeb Desert that was to bring great wealth and power to the Israelites. He vanquished (II Samuel 8:14) the Edomites, nomadic Semites who, along with Moabites and Ammonites, early in the thirteenth century B.C. drove out the Bedouins and took possession of what is now the country of Jordan. The Edomites possessed an advanced civilization and they dotted the land with well-built villages, mined copper and iron, were important traders. When Moses attempted to cross through Edom he was refused permission (Numbers 20:17; 21:22). Strong fortresses barred the way through Edom and through Moab to the north of it. The Israelites were compelled to detour around these kingdoms until they finally forced their way westward to the Jordan. Throughout much of their history, the relations between Israel and Edom were stormy, with warfare almost continuous. By his conquest of Edom, David extended the borders of the Israelites southward to the Gulf of Aqaba, an arm of the Red Sea. He gained more than a trade route and a seaport, for here were located the iron and copper mines that provided weapons and the fabled wealth of Solomon.

Solomon built smelters, a shipyard, and a port at Eziongeber (today known as Elath). Ruins of his smelters were unearthed north of Elath several years ago. They were located in a seemingly unlikely place, an inhospitable desert where water is scarce. There was a reason, though, for building them there. The smelters were an ingenious industrial enterprise that utilized some of the principles of the modern blast furnace. A constant and powerful wind roars down the valley where Solomon's smelters stood, and it acted as a bellows that kept the furnace fires burning at a high temperature. The thick walls of the smelters were pierced with an intricate system of holes and channels through which the wind entered.

Solomon became king in the year 961 B.C. and he reigned for thirty-nine years. The first book of Kings states that it was a period of peace and prosperity during which every man dwelt safely "under his vine and under his fig tree, from Dan even to Beer-sheba, all the days of Solomon" (I Kings 4:25). "Under his vine" is not just metaphor; it was possible to sit under a vine because grapes were often grown supported on the branches of fig trees. The name Solomon is derived from the Hebrew word for "peace," and Solomon indeed lived up to his name. Under him, Jerusalem became one of the most important cities of the Near East, and Solomon himself was declared "wiser than all men" (I Kings 4:31). He was supposed to have spoken more than three thousand proverbs and to have written more than a thousand songs, some of which have come down to us in the books of Proverbs and the Song of Solomon.

He could speak knowingly on any subject, and he was obviously an authority on natural history. The Bible states that he could lecture on "trees, from the cedar tree that is in Lebanon even unto the hyssop that springeth out of the wall: he spake also of beasts, and of fowl, and of creeping things, and of fishes" (I Kings 4:33). The cedar was the largest plant that Solomon could have known, and the little fragrant herb, the hyssop, was among the smallest. Today's garden flower known as the hyssop is not the plant Solomon spoke about, since it is not native to the eastern Mediterranean. Many scholars believe that the hyssop was one of the marjorams, members of the mint family. The marjoram he probably meant is low and shrubby, with clusters of white flowers, and, as Solomon stated, it is commonly found among rocks and in crevices in walls. When it grows in these unfavorable conditions, it is among the smallest flowering plants of the Holy Land, reaching only several inches in height.

The Bible describes Solomon as a gardener on a huge scale: "I planted me vineyards: I made me gardens and orchards, and I planted trees in them of all kinds of fruits: I made me pools of water, to water therewith the wood that bringeth forth trees" (Ecclesiastes 2:4-6). No one has yet found the exact location of Solomon's gardens, but they must have been quite close to the palace. A few miles outside of Jerusalem there are three large reservoirs that have traditionally been called the Pools of Solomon, and they may be the ones he built to provide water for his gardens.

Nor will anyone ever know for sure the exact layout of the gardens or the names of all the plants that grew in them. It is possible, however, to construct a general picture of these gardens, based on several hints in the Bible and on archaeological knowledge of other Holy Land gardens of that time. The garden actually was several different kinds of gardens close together. Each garden was probably rectangular in shape and walled, the sides of the walls masked by hedges.

Aside from a garden of olive trees, there was another garden for nut trees such as walnut, pistachio, and almond. The almond (which may have been derived from Hebrew words meaning "gift from God") was one of the most valued trees of the ancient world, both for the beauty of its flowers and for its fruit which could be eaten or pressed into oil. It was also associated with rebirth of life since it was the first of all the trees in the Holy Land to flower, producing blossoms often as early as January on branches still bare of leaves.

The most unusual of the gardens must have been the

one devoted to spices, for Solomon's far-flung trade with Arabia and India brought him many exotic plants. The eaglewood tree of India, for example, exuded from its trunk a fragrant gum called "aloes" in the Old Testament (the New Testament aloes came from a different plant, a succulent with thick fleshy leaves). The calamus, whose stem and leaves smelt strongly of ginger, was native to western India. One of the prizes of the spice garden was spikenard, which was found in the Himalaya Mountains of Asia. It is small and bears only inconspicuous flowers, but its hairy stem gives off a rich fragrance. The dried stems be-

Spikenard

came an important trade item in the ancient world. They were transported across Asia on camelback and stored in alabaster boxes to preserve their fragrance. That is the reason spikenard was extraordinarily expensive, as John points out when he states that Mary anointed the feet of Jesus with "a pound of ointment of spikenard, very costly" (John 12:3).

The wise Solomon admired what he considered to be wisdom in animals. It is interesting to note, though, that an animal we regard as exceedingly clever, the red fox, won no praise from Solomon. Every reference to it in the Bible is contemptuous. These small members of the dog family are naturally trusting, but as a result of their contact with man they have become wary and cunning. They have keen senses of sight, smell, and hearing, and they flee from danger at speeds up to thirty miles per hour. But they scavenged, like wild dogs and hyenas, in the Israelite cities, and that made them objects of contempt. They feed on almost anything: rodents, eggs, insects, grass. They even eat fruit, which may explain Solomon's reference to "the little foxes that spoil the vines" (Song of Solomon 2:15).

Solomon admired four creatures "which are little upon the earth, but they are exceeding wise" (Proverbs 30:24). The four are harvesting ants, conies, spiders, and locusts (the locust has already been discussed on page 62).

A proverb of Solomon quoted very often is: "Go to the ant, thou sluggard; consider her ways, and be wise: Which having no guide, overseer, or ruler, Provideth her meat in the summer, and gathereth her food in the harvest" (Proverbs 6:6-8). Until about a hundred years ago many people believed that Solomon's wisdom had finally failed him, for there was not a shred of evidence that ants gathered seeds during the harvest and stored them for use in the winter. In fact, so many doubts were raised about Solomon's wisdom on this score that in 1869 the president of London's distinguished Linnean Society suggested that the members should investigate the matter. One member finally discovered, in the south of France, ants carrying seeds. After much observation he confirmed that these seeds were indeed carried to underground granaries for storage. He learned that the ants not only carried back seeds that had fallen to the ground, but they also collected them from the plants themselves. Solomon had been proven correct after all.

Nowadays we know that harvesting ants are widespread around the world, almost wherever there are arid lands. In such an environment, seeds are an important food source. Like vitamin pills, they provide concentrated nutriment and they are easily stored. As Solomon wisely pointed out, most kinds of harvesting ants also eat "meat" when they can get it. But the small insects that ants might find in the desert are not a dependable food source, and so most kinds of harvesting ants rely mainly on their granaries. Some of the chambers in these underground granaries store enough seed to fill a milk bottle. One study in North America revealed that harvesting ants collected a total of fifteen million seeds a year from a single acre of land.

Harvesting ants have been studied closely in western North America where their mounds often are conspicuous features of the landscape. A medium-sized mound may have a diameter of about twelve feet and some mounds thirty-five feet across have been reported. No plants at all grow on the mounds since the ants completely remove every seedling that takes root. Such weeding is vital to the success of the storage operation. It prevents the roots of plants from growing into the underground chambers, and it also cuts down on moisture that might ruin the seeds by allowing molds to grow and rot them. Some species of harvesting ants also pave the mounds with small pieces of gravel that keep water off them. Despite these efforts, a downpour does occasionally wet the seeds. If that happens, the ants carry the seeds outdoors and lay them in the sun to dry.

Solomon stated that "the conies are but a feeble folk, yet make they their houses in the rocks" (Proverbs 30:26). The coney—or hyrax, as it should properly be called—at first glance somewhat resembles a plump rabbit, except that it lacks long ears. More careful inspection reveals that its feet end in tiny hoofs, and its closest living relative—unlikely as this may seem—is the elephant. One kind of hyrax

Hyrax (coney)

found in Africa lives in trees, but the kind that inhabits the Holy Land is a gregarious animal that lives in holes among rocks in deserts and mountains. Its colonies usually number up to fifty animals, and it is extremely agile at scampering over rocks. It can do this because of the peculiar construction of the soles of the feet. A special arrangement of muscles allows the soles to form a hollow air-tight cup which exerts suction when in contact with a flat surface. If a hyrax is shot while climbing up a rock, it may remain attached there, even though dead, held in place by the clinging power of the soles of its feet.

That small animals could so exploit rocks as places in which to live impressed Solomon, but he must have been amazed also at another aspect of their behavior. In the early morning and again in the evening, hyraxes leave the safety of their nests to browse on plants. At such times these "feeble folk" would be extremely vulnerable to predators—if they did not possess a warning system. At the approach of danger a hyrax sentry lets out a warning squeal or whistle which is echoed from animal to animal, giving them time to scamper back to the safety of the rocks.

The web of the spider must have seemed a particularly clever thing to Solomon, and he also was impressed that such small creatures could build a web as wonderfully constructed as his palace and actually invade it: "The spider taketh hold with her hands, and is in kings' palaces" (Proverbs 30:28). Spiders are not insects. Among other differences, they have four pairs of legs instead of the adult insect's three pairs. Nor are all spiders skilled weavers, although most kinds do construct some sort of a web. The silk does not emerge from the spider's "hands," as Solomon seemed to believe. Rather, six or eight tubelike spinnerets on the underside of the abdomen produce a liquid which hardens immediately on contact with the air into strands of silk which are then placed in position by the legs.

The entire web is really a projection of the spider's legs, allowing it to capture prey at a much farther distance than it ever could reach itself. If you destroy the web of a spider, it will rebuild an exact duplicate, and do so time after time, until it has temporarily exhausted its supply of silk. Usually each kind of web-making spider constructs a web in the same pattern and with the same series of steps as all other spiders of its species. Even a newly born spider, which has never seen a web before, builds a miniature exactly like that of its own species.

Among the most enterprising of Solomon's many ventures was his alliance with the Phoenicians. Phoenicians and Canaanites are the same people, but the Greeks, who traded with them, gave the name Phoenicia to the northern part of Canaan, the Mediterranean shore of the present-day Lebanon and Syria. The Bible never refers to the Phoenicians by name but instead calls them the people of Tyre, Sidon, or Gebal (Byblos), the three main cities from which the Phoenicians sent out trading voyages to all parts of the ancient world.

"Phoenicians" comes from the Greek word for "reddish-purple," which refers to the dye the Phoenicians prepared from species of murex, a carnivorous marine snail. The murex has a gland that secretes a strong-smelling fluid, milky-white in color, that serves as a defense against predators and as a narcotic to immobilize prey. When exposed to light and air, the fluid turns purple and is nearly ineradicable from fabrics. It was first used as a dye as early as 3,600 years ago, and by 3,000 years ago the Phoenicians had made dyeing into a remunerative business. As the numbers of the banded and spiny murex became almost completely depleted, the Phoenicians sent out ships to find new supplies. This was one reason for the founding of many Phoenician colonies, such as Carthage, throughout the Mediterranean.

Solomon negotiated an agreement with his Phoenician neighbor, King Hiram of Tyre, and in that way he obtained skilled workmen to build him a fleet of merchant ships. No one is certain exactly what these ships looked like, but they were probably a cross between the Phoenician battleship and merchant ship. The Bible refers to them as "Tarshish ships," probably because they were the kind the Phoenicians used on the long voyages to their ancient colony of Tarshish. Ezekiel refers (27:12) to the silver, iron, tin, and lead that came to Tyre from Tarshish, and the presence of these four metals has led scholars to believe that Tarshish was situated on the southern coast of Spain.

Solomon's fleet was based near his smelters, at Eziongeber on the Gulf of Aqaba. From there his ships sailed with metal and other items of trade to a place known as "Ophir." Its location has been much in dispute, and various scholars have placed it in North and East Africa, in Arabia, in India or Ceylon, and in Malaya. Some even thought it to be a legendary land—until there was recently discovered near the ancient port of Joppa (Jaffa) in Israel a Phoenician storage jar inscribed with the words "gold of Ophir." So we now know that such a place really existed, and that it was a source of gold.

Ophir very well may have been located in India or Ceylon, for the Bible states that the round-trip voyage took three years and that the ships brought back "gold, and silver, ivory, and apes, and peacocks" (I Kings 10:22). The Hebrew words for ivory, apes, and peacocks are very much the same as the words in the Tamil language spoken in southern India. The fleet may have brought back not only the cargo but also the names.

Ivory is the hard substance resembling bone that covers the teeth of several kinds of mammals, among them elephants, hippopotami, walruses, and whales. The ivory-bearing teeth of elephants are often called "tusks," and the ancient Hebrew writers revealed a knowledge of the true nature of ivory by using for it a word that meant "teeth" and not a word that indicated horns. The tusks of an elephant are the elongated upper front teeth, the only front teeth the elephant has, and they are used for fighting and for rooting up plants.

The African and the Asiatic are the two kinds of elephants in the world today, and they can be told apart easily enough. The Asiatic elephant, the one usually seen at the circus, has a high arch on its back, and a depression between its head and arching shoulders. The African elephant lacks both the arching back and the depression, but its ears are considerably larger. In Old Testament times the African elephant's range extended into northern Africa, but now it is found only south of the Sahara Desert. The Asiatic elephant also once lived much closer to the eastern Mediterranean than it does today—for written records from Egypt reveal that when a pharaoh conquered Syria about 3,400 years ago, he discovered a herd of elephants. Today most of the world's supply of ivory comes from the African

elephant, but in Solomon's time the main source was probably the Asiatic elephant.

No apes or monkeys are today native to the Holy Land,
nor is it believed that any were during the reign of Solomon. The Israelites, however, knew about monkeys from
their stay in Egypt, for the African baboon was sacred to
the god Thoth and was sometimes even kept as a pet. The
monkey brought back by Solomon's fleet possibly was the
rhesus, the kind most often seen in zoos and the one commonly used in medical research.

Peacocks, the last of the precious cargo from Ophir, are
among the most ornamented birds in the world. The shim-
mering royal-blue body feathers and huge fan-shaped tail
must have provided brilliant decoration for Solomon's
court. Although the common peacock, the one usually seen
in zoos, is native only to southern India and Ceylon, its
beauty has resulted in man's spreading it around the world.
It is quite hardy and can endure a wide range of climates
and living conditions. Only the male possesses the ornate
tail, and a male chick only several hours old raises its
tiny tail and struts like an adult. The unfurled fan of a fully
grown male has feathers five or six feet long. Each of these
bronze-green feathers is decorated with a richly colored
eyespot, and an outspread fan in all its glory looks like a
shield mounted with dozens of gleaming eyes.

The glitter of Solomon's court, his exotic gardens and
animals, his wisdom about wild things—these were famed
throughout the ancient world. But after his death in 922
B.C., the Israelites' power faded. It was at this time that
the great prophets arose, simple men who often illustrated
their sermons with their knowledge of the land and the lore
of the wild things that live on it.

VII. Wild Things of the Prophets

After the death of Solomon, the Israelites broke apart into two kingdoms: Israel, the northern ten tribes with the capital at Shechem, and Judah, the two tribes of Judah and Benjamin with the capital at Jerusalem. The crumbling empire of Solomon was attacked from the north by Syrians and from the south by Egyptians. Internally there was discord, and some of the people adopted the pagan animal worship of surrounding tribes. The disregard of the people for the ancient Hebrew ways was challenged by a succession of rugged and devout men, the prophets.

The prophet Amos, for example, used the lion to emphasize that his mission was to bring the Hebrews back to righteousness: "The lion hath roared, who will not fear? the Lord God hath spoken, who can but prophesy?" (Amos 3:8). No other wild animal is mentioned so often in the Bible as the lion, for it appears in thirty-one of the sixty-six books of the Old and New Testaments. Lions were still abundant in the Bible lands when Amos lived, and they ranged from Africa across the Near East to India. Now, though, they are extinct throughout most of this area. In the Holy Land itself, the lion was exterminated by about the time of the Crusades in the Middle Ages. It vanished from Egypt in the last century, and the last wild lion seen in the Near East was captured in Iran in 1923.

Hunting lions was an ancient sport in the Bible lands and many pictures show them being captured in nets and pits. Like many other Near Eastern monarchs, Darius, king of Persia, kept a den of lions—into which Daniel was cast. Daniel may have been extremely fortunate. If the lions had already been satisfied by a meal, he had little to fear from them. Once lions have fed, they are the laziest of the big cats, lying about virtually motionless for several days.

The prophet Jonah, legend has it, was swallowed by a "whale," but he survived the ordeal. The Bible, however, does not state that it was a whale at all, rather "a great fish" (Jonah 1:17). There has been considerable dispute about the identification of a sea creature large enough to swallow anything the size of a human. There seem to be two possibilities: the great fish was either a whale or a white shark.

Several kinds of whales are found in the Mediterranean, but only one of them—the sperm whale—has a gullet large enough for a grown man to pass through. Sperm whales, some of which grow as long as sixty-five feet, are fully able to swallow large prey. One harpooned sperm whale was found to contain in its stomach a shark almost ten feet long. There are, though, a few objections to accepting the sperm whale as the "great fish." Of course a whale is not a fish at all, rather a mammal adapted to life in the sea, like dolphins and seals. More important, sperm whales feed primarily on giant squids in the depths of the ocean, sometimes nosing down more than a mile to find them. It is unusual for them to prey on other large animals found in the sea, although occasionally they do so.

A more likely choice for the creature that swallowed Jonah is a true fish: the man-eating white shark which is often found in the Mediterranean. This shark is extremely large, occasionally up to sixty feet in length, and it is quite capable of swallowing a human. It also can store food in its belly for many days without digesting it, thus lending weight to the statement in the Bible that "Jonah was in the belly of the fish three days and three nights" (Jonah 1:17). The only difficulty is that it possesses a formidable array of teeth that would severely cut any animal passing through its jaws. There have been reports, though, of large sea creatures found intact in the stomachs of these sharks.

The warnings of the early prophets were not heeded, and disaster overtook Israel. There had arisen around the headwaters of the Tigris and Euphrates rivers a seminomadic people known as the Assyrians. Their name became a synonym for ruthlessness, for they built one of the most powerful war machines ever seen in the ancient world. Striking out in all directions, the Assyrians cut a wide swath of conquest across the entire Fertile Crescent from the Tigris to west of the Nile. In the year 721 B.C., the ten northern tribes of Israel were overrun. It was the custom of the Assyrians to uproot vanquished peoples and to re-settle them far from their homelands so that they would never again unite. The Ten Tribes of Israel were carried off to Assyria, and that is the last thing known about them. When the New World was discovered, there was a flurry of excitement that the American Indians might be the Ten Lost Tribes. Now, of course, it is known that the American Indians are descended from Asians who crossed over from Siberia to Alaska.

Like the Kingdom of Israel, the southern Kingdom of Judah also had its prophets who foretold doom unless the people put aside evil ways. The greatest of these prophets was Isaiah. He spoke of a future time of peace when "the desert shall rejoice, and blossom as the rose" (Isaiah 35:1). He did not mean our familiar rosebush, for the Hebrew word translated as rose refers to a plant with a bulbous root. There is some dispute among scholars as to exactly which plant that grows from a bulb was meant, but it probably was a narcissus. Most of the narcissi that bloom in our gardens in the spring nowadays come from Holland, but the plant was originally native to the deserts and dry hills of the Bible lands.

Jeremiah was another firebrand prophet of the declining years of Judah. He warned of the oncoming destruction by hostile empires, and he said that sinful people would become "meat for the fowls of the heaven, and for the beasts of the earth" (Jeremiah 7:33). By the "fowls" that would feast on the slain, he undoubtedly meant vultures. Unlike eagles and hawks, which usually kill living prey with their powerful talons, vultures feed on dead animals and they have only short, weak legs. The heads and necks of almost all vultures are naked of feathers, which is believed to be an adaptation to their feeding on carrion. Since the head comes in contact with diseased flesh of the prey, possible infection is avoided when the naked head and neck are exposed to the purifying rays of the sun.

An eagle can get a meal by a sudden surprise attack on a small animal, but a vulture searches for an animal that is already dead. Cooperation in finding carrion is essential, and once it is located, all vultures in the vicinity share. That is the reason a large number of vultures are often seen wheeling high in the air at the same time. When the keen eyes of one of them sight prey, this discovery is communicated to the other vultures by its descent toward earth. Vultures have extraordinary eyesight: one soaring nearly a mile above the earth can detect whether an animal is dead or merely resting.

The griffon is a huge vulture of the Holy Land, particularly abundant in mountainous areas. It is a majestic bird, with its head and neck bald of feathers but covered with a short white down, with its great wings nearly motionless as it soars for hours. Although it is large and powerful, it never kills its own prey, and it will not feed on any animal that still shows signs of life. It is a remarkably clean bird in its habits, bathing almost as frequently as it finds water and preening its feathers often.

The spectacular lammergeyer also is a mountainous bird, its nest usually situated in a cave on the side of a cliff or on a ledge protected by an overhang. The lammergeyer (sometimes called in the Bible the "ossifrage") is very distinctive, wearing tassels of feathers that hang from its beak like a long mustache or beard (and thus its other common

Eagle (top), Egyptian vulture (middle), griffon

name, bearded vulture). The lammergeyer feeds almost exclusively on the marrow inside the bones of animals already picked clean by other kinds of vultures. Lammergeyer means "lamb vulture" and indeed it often does feed on the carcasses of lambs. It swallows the small bones, but it shatters the large ones by dropping them from great heights onto rocks.

The "beasts of the earth" that Jeremiah said would appear after the destruction of Judah probably referred to wild dogs and hyenas. Today the dog is known as a faithful domesticated animal, but during biblical times packs of snarling wild dogs foraged through the city streets and even dug up corpses to feed on them. Dogs are treated with great contempt not only in the Bible but also in the writings of other peoples in the Near East. One kind of wild dog found in the Holy Land is the golden jackal, its color a dirty yellow mixed with red and black. It usually travels in small packs, feeding on any animals it can catch.

Looking at a picture of a hyena, you might think that it

Striped hyena

is nothing more than a mangy dog. But a hyena is not a dog, and the two animals are not even closely related. The hyena is a specialized scavenger that possesses an extremely heavy skull, powerful jaw muscles, and massive teeth. These characteristics are a clue to its way of life. It does not compete with vultures for carrion, but rather uses its powerful jaws to crush the bones of animals that have already been plucked clean by the vultures. The striped hyena, the one found in the Holy Land, is smaller than the hyena of the African plains and it is less aggressive. Yet it was the most feared and detested of all animals in the ancient world because of its habit of digging up graves. The Egyptians lacked this aversion to hyenas, for they partially domesticated them as a source of food. Young hyenas are easy to tame and quickly become attached to their masters.

Jeremiah made the earliest statements about bird migration that have survived: "Yea, the stork in the heaven knoweth her appointed times; and the turtle and the crane and the swallow observe the time of their coming" (Jeremiah 8:7). Long before man used the Near East as a crossroads for his caravans, birds flew over it on invisible migration highways. Of the birds named by Jeremiah in the above passage, the turtledove has already been discussed on page 21 in connection with Noah. The white stork is unmistakable in flight because of its sharply pointed head and extended neck, long dangling legs, and slowly flapping wings. Flocks of several thousand of them pass over the Holy Land at a time. One mass flight in this century in the southern part of the Holy Land was estimated to be more than a mile wide and several miles long. The flights in biblical times were even more spectacular,

White stork

for the white stork has now become quite rare in many parts of its range. The white stork spends the warm part of the year in Europe and during the autumn it migrates to Africa. In Germany and in Holland it is regarded as a bird of good fortune, and many houseowners put platforms on their roofs in the hope storks will use them for nesting. The birds are faithful to these nesting areas. Parent birds return year after year to the same rooftops, and young birds build their first nests in the vicinity of the one from which they took flight.

The crane is tall and stately with a wingspread of about eight feet. It is the largest migrating bird to fly over the Holy Land. Its mass flights are dramatic because the birds number in the thousands, and also because they make a trumpeting sound that rends the air. The trumpeting probably serves to keep the birds together. One of the loudest sounds made by any bird, it is produced by the crane's extremely long windpipe which is coiled like a French horn.

Jeremiah's reference to the swallow in the above passage for a long time posed a problem for biblical scholars. They wondered why Jeremiah should have selected a nonmigratory species when there were so many migratory ones to choose from. The confusion seems to have resulted from a mistranslation. Instead of the swallow, Jeremiah apparently meant the migratory swift, and recent translations of the Bible substitute the name of this bird for the swallow. Swifts migrate to the tropics in winter, traveling by day in loose flocks and roosting at night in caves, hollow trees, and chimneys. It is understandable that translators should have made a mistake, for the swift and the swallow are very similar in appearance and lead much the same sort of lives.

Both pursue insects on the wing, both have forked tails, and both are superb aerialists. But the swift is related to hummingbirds, and the swallow to martins.

The speediest birds in the world are some Asiatic swifts whose maximum speed has been estimated at two hundred miles an hour, although this figure is probably exaggerated. Swifts fly not only fast but far, and some travel more than two hundred miles in a day just to obtain food. They are the very embodiment of life in the air. Most of their waking hours are spent aloft, pursuing insects on the wing. In fact, their feet are small, weak, and useless for walking or even for perching on branches.

No one in the ancient world seemed to know for sure where migrating birds came from, why they left, or where they went to. There were plenty of theories, though. Aristotle, the Greek philosopher, stated that birds did not fly to a different place at all—they merely disappeared from sight by hibernating in caves or in the ground. This idea was ridiculed for more than two thousand years, in fact until 1946 when scientists discovered that a species of poorwill in California spends the entire winter in a state of torpor in a rock crevice. It remains completely inactive for nearly three months. The poorwill's digestive system shuts down, its breathing virtually stops, and its body temperature falls from a normal 102 degrees F. to 65 degrees. All through the cold winter it sleeps in its crevice in the canyon walls, awakening in the spring at a time when insect food is again available. Now it has been learned that a few other birds spend part of the winter in torpor, including some swifts that live in northern Europe.

These birds, though, are exceptions, for many kinds do

Cranes

undertake long migrations. Knowledge about migration has come largely from the worldwide cooperation of birdbanders who slip small identifying metal rings on the legs of captured birds and then release them. The place and date of the banding are recorded. When afterward the bird is trapped, shot, or found dead, a clue to its migration has been obtained. In the United States and Canada, banders ring more than 600,000 birds each year. Of the more than eleven million birds they have banded, almost a million have been recovered, a remarkably high percentage of success. Other countries also have banding programs: Germany has banded nearly four million birds, England and

Swifts

Russia about two million each, and even little Switzerland about half a million.

Assyria rose rapidly to power—and its decline was just as rapid. New empires were on the ascendancy. A nation known as the Medes arose east of the Tigris River. And the Babylonians once again strode to power across the Near Eastern stage. The Medes and the Babylonians formed an alliance and dismembered the Assyrian Empire, the Babylonians claiming the Holy Land. The armies of King Nebuchadnezzar of Babylonia overran Judah and, after two years, finally conquered Jerusalem itself. In the year 587 B.C. the Holy City lay in ruins, and its people were led off to captivity in Babylon. Their name changed to Jews (from the Hebrew *Yehudi*, which means "belonging to the tribe of Judah"), they kept alive their faith and their way of life during the years of exile.

Ezekiel was the great prophet during the Babylonian exile, and he often spoke knowingly about the land and its life. For a long time scholars disputed about what animal he meant by "the great dragon" (Ezekiel 29:3). Some believed that it was merely an imaginary monster, others that a serpent or other real animal was meant. There was no proof one way or the other until archaeologists excavated ancient Babylon early in this century. They dug out of the rubble the remains of an enormous gate, ordered built by Nebuchadnezzar himself. The ruins of the Ishtar Gate, as it is called, still rise to a height of about forty feet, and it must have been even higher in ancient times. It was decorated with rows of animal sculptures, at least 575 figures in all, made out of mud brick and then enameled with

Sirrush

brilliant colors. One of the animals was a fantastic beast: the Sirrush or Dragon of Babylon.

The Sirrush was a combination serpent, cat, and eagle. Its head, body, and tail were covered with snakelike scales. Its forelegs resembled those of a lion, and its hind legs ended in talons like those of an eagle. No one knows for certain why the Sirrush was placed on the gates, but Nebuchadnezzar ordered these words inscribed on it: "Fierce bulls and grim dragons I put and thus supplied the gates with such overflowing rich splendor that all humanity may view it with wonderment." It is possible, too, that the figures were intended to impress or even to frighten the Medes and Persians. So although actual dragons never existed, sculptured figures of them must have been seen by Ezekiel during the exile in Babylon.

The Ishtar Gate was not the only thing of splendor in this imposing city. Excavations have revealed magnificent broad avenues, lined with palaces, temples, and stately homes. One of the main avenues led from the gate through the city to the most important temple, the ziggurat or Tower of Babel. Along this main avenue also was located one of the Seven Wonders of the Ancient World: the Hanging Gardens of Babylon. The gardens, or what is left of their foundations, have been brought into the light again from under more than two thousand years of rubble. The gardens were said to "hang" because they sprouted from a high man-made mountain that was terraced, each terrace planted with trees and flowers. Water to irrigate the plants was pumped from wells in the foundation itself or from the nearby Euphrates River. Artificial brooks and waterfalls probably also ran down the sides of the mountain.

Job is thought to have lived in the Arabian Desert, somewhere between Babylon and the Holy Land, during the years of the exile. He was the great naturalist of the Old Testament and he displayed a deep knowledge of and an observant eye for the world around him. "Speak to the earth, and it shall teach thee," he advises (Job 12:8). He followed his own advice, for he describes precisely the habits of mammals, the ways of birds, the patterns in the skies, the rains and the floods. He speaks knowingly of the various trees that grow along the streams, the papyrus in the marshes, the thorny shrubs of the desert.

He was a keen watcher of the skies. In Chapter 9 he refers to "Arcturus, Orion, and the Pleiades, and the chambers of the south." He was aware that the stars are not scattered at random in the night sky but are fixed in unchanging patterns, one of which is the Zodiac. "Zodiac" is derived from the same Greek word as zoo, and it means "circle of animals." The Zodiac is an imaginary belt across the sky consisting of twelve groups of stars—constellations, or "chambers," as Job called them—through which the sun and the moon seem to pass. Each constellation appeared to the ancients to represent the figure of some animal or a mythical being usually associated with animals.

In the passage quoted above, Arcturus is the brightest star in the constellation Boötes, also sometimes called "The Bear Driver" or "The Herdsman." Orion the Hunter is a prominent winter constellation, and he is sometimes visualized as holding a lion's skin in his hand. The Pleiades are a cluster of stars—six of them when viewed with the naked eye, but numbering thousands when seen through a telescope—in the shoulder of Taurus the Bull. (Taurus is the only one of these three constellations that is in the Zodiac.)

Observations about birds abound in Job, and none is more precise than the word-picture of the ostrich: it "leaveth her eggs in the earth, and warmeth them in dust, And forgetteth that the foot may crush them, or that the wild beast may break them. She is hardened against her young ones, as though they were not hers: her labor is in vain without fear; Because God hath deprived her of wisdom, neither hath he imparted to her understanding" (Job 39: 14-17).

The ostrich was abundant in the Arabian Desert in Job's

time but it became extinct there during World War II (it has very nearly been wiped out in Egypt also). As Job states, the female lays her eggs, usually about a dozen of them, in a cavity scooped out of the desert. The incubation period is a long one, about a month and a half, but the ostrich does not have to sit on the eggs all of the time. During the day she can leave them because they are kept warm by the heat of the sun. So Job is correct in saying that the ostrich abandons her eggs during the day, but he wrongly condemns her for it.

Job also condemns the ostrich for deserting the eggs when danger threatens. It is true that in times of danger the ostrich flees the nest, but her flight is actually an important way of protecting the eggs against predators. The eggs, and the chicks as well, are camouflaged. So the only clue a predator might have to their location is the sight of the parent ostrich sitting on her nest. When an ostrich flees from her nest, she is really diverting the predator and in that way saving her young. This tactic exposes the adult bird to little danger since it can run at a speed of nearly forty miles an hour, and can even outdistance pursuing horses.

Job further accuses the female of being hardened against the chicks "as though they were not hers." Here again he has made an accurate observation, but once more he has drawn the wrong conclusions. As soon as the chicks hatch out, the male ostrich takes over the complete charge of their care. There is nothing "hardened" in this behavior; it is just that the habits of ostriches are different from those of humans.

Job is also correct in his low estimation of the ostrich's

intelligence, although it is not so stupid that it hides its head in the sand in time of danger, as some people believe. The legend, though, does have some basis in fact. A young ostrich, when threatened, extends its neck straight out along the ground and crouches motionless in an effort to become less visible. The ostrich is a primitive bird that relies heavily on blind instinct, displaying little of the intelligence seen in more advanced birds such as woodpeckers. For all its great size, its brain is only the size of a walnut.

The ostrich's lack of wisdom and understanding is compensated for by numerous physical adaptations that aid its survival in the desert. It can detect danger at a great distance because its huge eyes are about eight feet above the surface of the ground, set atop a very long neck that resembles a periscope. The ostrich can outrun any animal that threatens it. It usually tries to flee from danger, but if it has to stand and fight, it can give murderous kicks with its massive legs, tipped with claws that resemble hoofs. It can survive in the desert for days without water, and it can make do with almost any desert plant for food.

In a long series of verses in Chapter 40, Job describes an animal he calls a "behemoth," but it is unmistakably a hippopotamus. There may have been hippopotami inhabiting the Jordan Valley in biblical times, although none are found there now, and they are today extinct north of the Sudan in Africa as well. The Hebrews undoubtedly knew them in Egypt, and it is even possible that Job's behemoth is derived from the Egyptian name for this animal —pehemout, which means "ox of the water." Job's description of the hippopotamus' size and power is exaggerated,

Ostrich

but not unduly so when you consider that its head alone may weigh a ton and that only the elephant, of all terrestrial mammals, is larger. Job also declares that the hippopotamus "drinketh up a river." The hippopotamus is very much a water animal. The young are born under water and they can swim before they can walk. An adult hippo usually remains in the water during the day, but it emerges onto land at night to feed. It may travel fifteen miles in a single night, although it seldom ventures more than a few hundred yards from water.

There is much less certainty about the identification of the "leviathan" described at great length in all thirty-four verses of Chapter 41. Commentators on the Bible disagree as to whether the leviathan was a crocodile, a whale, or even some mythical animal. It appears most likely that Job had in mind the crocodile, although an exaggerated one that spouts fire from its mouth. Other portions of his description, though, are accurate. As Job points out, this reptile is covered with scales so tough and so closely overlapping that it is difficult to spear one. The crocodile's teeth are indeed terrifying, and the jaws so strong that "who can open the doors of his face?" (Job 41:14). In thrashing with its tail when attacked, the crocodile does "maketh the deep to boil like a pot" (Job 41:31).

The ancient Hebrews knew the crocodile as an inhabitant of the Nile, the Jordan, and several other rivers in the Bible lands. The last crocodiles in the Jordan River were killed off about a hundred years ago. A few survived in the northern part of Israel until the last of them died about 1920 when their swamp was drained to build a modern settlement. Even the crocodiles in Africa are disappearing rapidly, and today you rarely see the vast number of twenty-foot monsters that once crowded the river banks. Although the crocodile's scales are as formidable as Job describes, they are no protection against modern high-powered rifles.

Job's fortitude in the face of adversity was duplicated, on a larger scale, by the Jews held captive in Babylon. Their period of exile ended when Cyrus, king of Persia, conquered Babylon in 539 B.C. and a year later decreed that all of its enslaved peoples, among them the Jews, could return to their homeland. At first only about forty thousand of them returned. They found their former great cities falling into ruin and other peoples occupying the Holy Land. The Edomites had moved up from the south and had settled the hills of Hebron. The Samaritans, a people formed from the remnants of numerous nations that had been conquered by the Assyrians and resettled in Samaria, occupied the northern part of the Holy Land. The Philistines and the Phoenicians along the coast had grown powerful. A new Temple was erected in Jerusalem in 516 B.C. to replace the one destroyed by the Babylonians, but it was a simple structure compared to the luxurious Temple of Solomon.

The Jews never again became a mighty people in the ancient world, except for the short reign of the Maccabees between 166 and 63 B.C. But the restored little Kingdom of Judah was soon to nourish a new faith that would spread over the Bible lands and over the entire world.

VIII. A Star in the East

In the five centuries between the rebuilding of the Temple at Jerusalem and the birth of Jesus, the Bible lands ceased to be the focal point for the ancient world. New empires arose, and this time they came from Europe. First the Greeks, then the Romans, overran the Bible lands. The Near Eastern peoples saw their land despoiled of trees and precious metals to supply the conquerors. What forests had survived were cut down. The wilderness gave way to fields, the wild beasts were largely replaced by domesticated animals. That is why most of the references in the New Testament to the natural world are to familiar farm plants and animals rather than to the wilderness that existed earlier.

Jesus is the Greek form of the Hebrew name Joshua. We reckon dates from the supposed year of his birth—A.D. 1—but this date was arrived at by a European abbot six centuries later. The abbot had available only the fragmentary scholarship of his time, and he almost certainly erred in his calculations. We still use his date for our calendar, but modern scholarship indicates that Jesus was born several years earlier, probably in 6 B.C.

About the time of the birth of Jesus in Bethlehem, a peaceful town on a hill six miles south of Jerusalem, a phenomenon occurred in the night sky. There has been considerable dispute about what this bright Star of Bethlehem may have been, and there is still no agreement among scholars. The great astronomer Kepler showed that a most unusual event in the heavens occurred just previous to Jesus' birth. The planets Jupiter and Saturn seemed to meet in the constellation Pisces, "The Fish," to form a single brilliant object. Such a conjunction, as this apparent meeting of planets is called by astronomers, occurs on an average of once in about eight hundred years—yet Kepler stated that it took place three times shortly before Jesus' birth. Jupiter and Saturn were particularly important in the Bible lands, since Jupiter was regarded as the royal planet and Saturn as the planet that protected Israel. Other astronomers believe that the Star of Bethlehem was actually the planet Venus which sometimes becomes a particularly brilliant "morning star," so bright that even the full light of the rising sun cannot outshine it.

Whatever the astronomical phenomenon was exactly, it did not go unobserved in the ancient home of astronomy, Mesopotamia. The Wise Men or Magi who saw the star and believed that it heralded the birth of Jesus were probably astronomers. "Magus" was a Persian word that referred to the priests there, and from it we have obtained

Frankincense (left) and myrrh

our English word "magic." In the ancient world the priests who could predict eclipses and the motions of the planets must indeed have seemed to possess magical powers. The Bible itself does not state the number of Magi who followed the Star to Bethlehem, nor does it tell much about them. The Christian tradition that they were three kings did not arise until about seven hundred years afterward.

Matthew states (2:11) that the Magi brought gifts of gold, frankincense, and myrrh. Frankincense and myrrh are spices, and their rarity in the ancient world is confirmed by their being grouped with gold. Nowadays people do not place a very high value on spices, but in biblical times the burning of fragrant substances was believed to heal and also to ward off evil. Aside from the aromatic smoke given off by these two spices, they were both used extensively by the Greeks and Romans in prescriptions for many kinds of medicines.

Frankincense and myrrh are gums obtained by piercing the bark of several kinds of trees that grow in the dry country of Arabia, Ethiopia, and Somalia. The frankincense tree is large, and related to the terebinth or turpentine tree; the myrrh is low and scrubby, with many branches. Both have become very rare, and the frankincense tree is virtually extinct in those areas. Frankincense, though, is still widely used by the Arabs who obtain it from similar trees which grow in the Malay Archipelago. The incense is brought from Malaya to the Near East by Asiatic Arabs who make pilgrimages to the holy city of Mecca in Saudi Arabia.

The center of the ancient spice trade was Sheba in what is now Yemen. When the Queen of Sheba traveled to Jerusalem to see for herself the splendors of Solomon's court, the Israelites were astonished by the vast quantities of precious spices she brought with her. In the time of Solomon, and for four hundred years after, Sheba was a rich and fertile country. Archaeologists have dug under the dunes of Marib, the capital of ancient Sheba, and unearthed ruins of huge temples and buildings, all of great splendor and beauty. A gigantic dam furnished water for the spice plants, and the whole kingdom must have been one sweet-smelling garden. Then the dam burst and the desert invaded the land, making it the desolate place it is today. So the Sabaeans, as the people of Sheba were called, became traders in spices instead of producers of them. At the time of Jesus they were still the richest Arab tribe because they controlled caravan routes that led to all parts of the ancient world in quest of spices. The Sabaeans' monopoly of the spice trade lasted until about five centuries ago when Portuguese mariners found a sea route to the spice lands of Asia around the southern tip of Africa.

Because Herod ordered the slaughter of young Jewish children, Mary and Joseph fled to Egypt with the child Jesus. The Egypt in which Jesus found shelter was much different from the proud and mighty nation that his ancestors Abraham and Moses had known. The glory that had been Egypt was gone. The flourishing cities through which pharaohs once rode in pomp were decaying, the great pyramids and temples were crumbling. Egypt was now a mere curiosity for wealthy Greek and Roman tourists to visit. They sailed up the Nile, looked at the Sphinx and the pyramids, and they even scratched their names on the walls of temples.

Joseph and Mary returned from Egypt some time after the death of Herod in 4 B.C. and made their home in Nazareth, a town in Galilee. The name Nazareth is derived from Hebrew words that mean "consecrated people" because this town was noted for clinging to the ancient laws and customs of the Hebrews. Hebrew was still the language of the places of worship, but outside of them the people spoke a dialect known as Aramaic. They also carried on conversations in Greek. It was not the classical language of Homer and the heroes, but a dialect known as Koine, the language in which the bulk of the New Testament was written. Undoubtedly Jesus learned to speak all three languages.

The Bible narrates little of Jesus' life until about A.D. 27 when he went to Bethany Beyond Jordan on the eastern side of the Jordan River, so called to distinguish it from another Bethany on the western side. There John the Baptist was baptizing large numbers of people in the waters of the Jordan as a symbol of spiritual cleansing. The young Jesus came to John, asking to be washed clean in these waters.

Luke reports (3:22) that as Jesus was being baptized, the spirit of God "descended in a bodily shape like a dove upon him." A dove with an olive leaf in its bill had been a symbol of forgiveness for Noah. Now at the Jordan the dove became a new symbol of love. Later the dove came to symbolize the Christian Church itself. When a new saint is canonized at St. Peter's Church in Rome, cages containing doves are carried to the pope.

After the baptism, Jesus traveled south to the Wilderness of Judaea, which lies to the west of the Dead Sea. The naturally dry climate of Judaea is made even more inhospitable by its porous rocks, which allow rainwater to sink into the ground before it can benefit plants. Today trees are almost totally absent there, and grass sprouts from the barren land only during the two or three wettest months each winter. Its barrenness, though, was not so severe in Jesus' time. Shrubs once grew in Judaea, but they have been cut down since New Testament times. Many parts of Judaea will support trees if they are planted there again, and in some of the bleakest areas I have seen new forests sprouting out of this eroded land.

Jesus spent forty days in the wilderness of Judaea, then made his way back to Galilee, where he began his ministry. His preaching contained unforgettable sayings and stories, known as parables. Since he spoke primarily to the humble people who labored on the land and were familiar with the animals and plants around them, his parables are resplendent with images of the natural world.

Typical of the parables is Jesus' story of the Good Shepherd, told in the tenth chapter of John. Jesus knew that his audience was familiar with the problems of caring for flocks and herds. So he told a simple story about how sheep recognize their master but flee from a stranger. Jesus compares himself to the good shepherd who "giveth his life for the sheep" (John 10:11). The hireling, however, does not think of protecting his flock and he flees at the approach of the wolf.

The wolf is mentioned numerous times in the Bible. It is almost always a symbol of treachery, as in Jesus' warning: "Beware of false prophets, which come to you in sheep's clothing, but inwardly they are ravening wolves" (Matthew 7:15). Many naturalists believe that the gray wolf of Europe and Asia possesses different habits from the same species in North America. There is a long history of documented attacks by wolves on humans in the Old World. There have been reports of gray wolf attacks on people in North America also. The U.S. Fish and Wildlife Service carefully investigated all such reports over a twenty-five-year period and concluded that not one of them was true. Since then, however, there have been a handful of cases, but it is believed that these animals were suffering from rabies.

Carob tree (locust)

In Jesus' moving parable of the Prodigal Son, the younger of two sons squandered his half of an inheritance. He became so poor that he would willingly have "filled his belly with the husks that the swine did eat" (Luke 15:16). Husks were the pods from the carob tree, also commonly called the locust, which were fed to farm animals. (Many scholars now believe that the "locust"—Matthew 3:4—which John the Baptist ate in the wilderness was not the insect

137

but rather the pod of this tree. For this reason the carob is sometimes called the "St. John's Bread tree.")

The carob grows beans in pods that somewhat resemble our green peas. Today in the Near East the pods provide fodder for animals and food for the very poor people, although in Jesus' time humans did not eat them unless they were as famished as the Prodigal Son. A large carob, one about thirty feet tall, might produce as much as three thousand pounds of pods each year. Carob seeds were brought to North America in the last century and were distributed throughout the southern states for ornamental plantings. They are not widely grown there today, but occasionally you come across a large carob in the warmer parts of the South.

The plant world provided many other subjects for Jesus. In the parable of the tares and the wheat (Matthew 13: 24-29), tares refers to a variety of rye grass that was the most troublesome weed of the wheat fields. A servant asks whether the tares should be weeded out of the field, but the master tells him: "Nay; lest while ye gather up the tares, ye root up also the wheat with them" (Matthew 13: 29). Tares are almost indistinguishable from wheat until fully grown. The point of this parable is that any attempt to weed out the tares would inevitably result in a loss of wheat plants, just as in a punishment of the guilty, innocent people might suffer also.

In speaking of the small beginnings that lead to great growth, Jesus uses the example of little seeds that sprout almost unnoticed until they spring out of the ground as sturdy growths. He speaks of "a grain of mustard seed . . . Which indeed is the least of all seeds: but when it is grown, it is the greatest among herbs, and becometh a tree, so that the birds of the air come and lodge in the branches thereof" (Matthew 13:31-32). Indeed, few plants in the Holy Land have seeds smaller than the mustard. As Jesus points out, the mustard nevertheless often grows as large as a tree, reaching a height of about fifteen feet in parts of the Holy Land. The mustard was widely cultivated in the Near East for the flavor of its seed. Our modern mustard is made from these seeds after they have been ground to a fine powder.

Jesus often illustrates his parables with references to the grapevine, so widely cultivated in the Holy Land that it was known to all listeners. He uses it to symbolize his relationship to his disciples: "I am the vine, ye are the branches: He that abideth in me, and I in him, the same bringeth forth much fruit: for without me ye can do nothing" (John 15:5). The grapevine is one of the very first plants mentioned in the Bible and it appears some two hundred times in both the Old and the New Testament. Jesus' listeners understood that the branches of the grapevine, no matter how well tended, could not bear grapes if the main stem through which the branches received sustenance was severed.

Jesus preached the Sermon on the Mount on a hillside clothed with the wildflowers that had sprung out of the ground after the winter rains. In trying to explain to his listeners the futility of piling up wealth, he must have looked about him and seen that his lesson could be illustrated by the very flowers at his feet. "Consider the lilies of the field," he said, "how they grow; they toil not, neither do they spin: And yet I say unto you, That even Solomon in all his glory was not arrayed like one of these" (Matthew 6:28-29).

The lily of the field is the best-known flower of the New

Testament, and also the one about which there has been the most dispute among scholars. Many people incorrectly believe that the flower meant was the one we nowadays call the Madonna lily. This belief stems from paintings of the Madonna by Renaissance artists who depicted this lily, but who had never visited the Holy Land or even knew much about its plant life. The Madonna lily almost certainly was not the flower called "lily of the field," for it was not introduced into the Holy Land from northern Syria until after the time of Jesus. Most authorities now agree that Jesus meant the brightly colored anemone, also known as the windflower. At the time of the year that Jesus delivered the Sermon on the Mount, anemones carpet the land with great splashes of color. Their scarlet blossoms would have caught his eye as he spoke, for they are brighter than any flower of that season.

Another of Jesus' teachings that for a long time confused scholars was: "It is easier for a camel to go through the eye of a needle, than for a rich man to enter into the kingdom of God" (Matthew 19:24). Most people have visualized the needle as an ordinary sewing needle—in which case it would be utterly impossible for a rich man ever to enter heaven. Since Jesus also preached that a rich man under certain conditions might enter heaven, he must have intended something else besides the eye of a sewing needle. Archaeological excavations have now clarified the meaning. The ancient cities of the Near East usually were walled, and at night the gates were closed for protection against invaders. In case any of the citizens were unable to return before nightfall, one small opening was left in the gate, and this opening was known as "the needle's eye." It was so low and so narrow that a camel, laden with riches, could never fit through. Only when the owner left the load outside the gate could the camel, with its head bent low, squeeze through. The meaning of the teaching is now apparent. A rich man could enter the kingdom of heaven— but only if he first cast off his wordly goods and, like the camel squeezing through the needle's eye, bowed his head in humility.

As Jesus traveled around the countryside preaching, he entered Jericho. There a rich man named Zacchaeus wanted to catch a glimpse of Jesus, but to see him he had to climb a sycomore tree (Luke 19:4). The sycomore, not to be confused with the sycamore, is an inferior kind of fig tree that has traditionally been a food of impoverished people in the Near East. Thus the rich man was forced to rely on the tree that was a symbol for poverty. The sycomore, by the way, is an easy tree to climb since its main trunk divides into a shower of thick branches only a short distance above the ground.

Disregarding warnings by his disciples that he avoid Jerusalem, Jesus entered the city just before the Feast of Passover. He traveled from Bethany—which means "house of dates"—and made his triumphal entry amidst the waving of long fronds from date palms. To this day, Christians commemorate Jesus' arrival in Jerusalem as Palm Sunday. The date palm still flourishes along the coastal plain of the Holy Land, and in biblical times it was so common in the Jordan Valley also that Jericho was called "the city of palm trees" (Deuteronomy 34:3). The date palm is usually regarded as a typical desert tree, but that is not true at all.

It requires an abundant supply of water and so it grows only in oases or near springs. In the ancient world it was a symbol of hope because a weary traveler in the desert, seeing one in the distance, knew that he was approaching water.

John states (12:13) that the crowds of people who met Jesus "took branches of palm trees"—but the palm tree actually has no branches. Most people believe that the extremely long leaves, in some species of palms twenty feet in length, are branches, but they are wrong. The entire

Date palm

"branch" is really the midrib of a single, deeply-notched leaf that is connected directly to the trunk.

The date palm, native to the lands bordering the Mediterranean, is the oldest known species of tree to be cultivated by man. Its association with man has extended over so long a period of time that it is never found growing in the wild. Although most of the higher plants are pollinated by insects or by wind, the date palm no longer bears fruit unless it is pollinated by the hand of man. The grower must remove a pollinating strand from the flower of one tree and insert it into the flower of a nearby tree. This partnership of man and date palm is of such antiquity that it is even depicted in Assyrian sculpture.

The planting of a date palm is an act of faith in the future, for it requires much perseverance to grow one to maturity. The soil must be carefully prepared, the desert sands must be kept from burying the young growth, a constant supply of water must be furnished. Even if the seedling survives, it does not bear well until it attains an age of several decades. Thereafter, though, it may give an annual crop of four hundred pounds and bear for one to two centuries, an inheritance down to the seventh or eighth generation. A grove of date palms is indeed a valued legacy, for every part of the tree provides benefits: the fruit for food, the wood for fuel, the leaves for thatching, the outside fibers for weaving into rope.

After the Last Supper, Jesus spent his last night of freedom in the Garden of Gethsemane on the slopes of the Mount of Olives. Gethsemane was not a flower garden as we might visualize one today. Rather, its name means "olive presses," and it was a place where olive trees grew particularly thick and where their oil was pressed from the fruit. In Jesus' time the Mount of Olives was covered with a luxuriant growth of these trees, and the inhabitants of Jerusalem often retired there to seek relief from the sun. But about forty years after Jesus spent the night on the Mount, the Romans cut down all of the olive trees. Today olive trees again grow there, and it is possible that some of them have sprung from the same roots as the trees under which Jesus rested. Cutting down an olive tree actually rejuvenates it, for new vigorous sprouts are sent up by the roots. The roots are extremely long-lived and it is almost impossible to kill an olive tree merely by chopping it down. The olive was the symbol of peace in the ancient world, and so it was fitting that it was associated with Jesus who was also known as the Prince of Peace.

On the way to Gethsemane, Jesus told his disciple Peter that "this day, even in this night, before the cock crow twice, thou shalt deny me thrice" (Mark 14:30). The roosters first crowed about midnight, and they were so punctual that Roman soldiers used the sound as a signal for changing the guard. The roosters crowed a second time about three o'clock in the morning, in that way awakening the second watch.

Until recent decades, when new breeds of chickens were developed, the rooster was little different from its wild pheasant ancestor, the red jungle fowl found from Pakistan to Java. The red jungle fowl much resembles the barnyard chicken both in appearance and in habits, except that it still possesses the power of flight. Like the chicken, it travels in flocks and, when disturbed, it calls noisily. Jesus refers to a habit of both the jungle fowl and the chicken in time of danger when he says: "how often would I have gathered thy children together, even as a hen gathereth her chickens under her wings" (Matthew 23:37). Archaeologists have found evidence that the chicken may have been domesticated as early as 5,200 years ago in India. The birds were raised at that time for the sport of cock-fighting, and

Jungle fowl, ancestor of chicken

they were not bred for food until several centuries before the time of Jesus.

Jesus could have escaped the Roman soldiers by fleeing eastward from Gethsemane, but he remained until his betrayal by Judas. After he was condemned to death, he was mocked by the Roman soldiers and made to wear a crown of thorns: "And the soldiers . . . platted a crown of thorns, and put it about his head" (Mark 15:16-17). There has been considerable dispute about exactly which shrub the soldiers used to make the crown, and about half a dozen different kinds have been suggested. One thing, though, is certain. The shrub commonly known as "crown of thorns," grown in many European and American gardens, could not possibly be the one mentioned in the Bible. This plant is native to the island of Madagascar and it was unknown in the Holy Land in Jesus' time. Many authorities now believe that the crown was made from a straggly shrub often called the Jerusalem thorn. It grows abundantly around Jerusalem, and its twigs are flexible enough to be woven.

On the morning of the crucifixion, Jesus was marched to a hill called Golgotha, derived from an Aramaic word that means "skull." Tradition places the site of the crucifixion where Christendom's holiest shrine, the Church of the Holy Sepulchre, built in the fourth century, now stands. The Roman soldiers gave Jesus "vinegar to drink mingled with gall" (Matthew 27:34). Some scholars believe that gall was the juice from a poppy, which has the effect of making the drinker insensitive to pain. No one, however, can be certain, for Mark says that the potion offered Jesus consisted of "wine mingled with myrrh" (Mark 15:23).

After the crucifixion there was brought "a mixture of

Jerusalem thorn

myrrh and aloes, about an hundred pound weight. Then took they the body of Jesus, and wound it in linen clothes with the spices, as the manner of Jews is to bury" (John 19:39-40). Myrrh was one of the main ingredients in the spices used in the purification of the dead. Aloes, when referred to in the New Testament, was different from that in the Old. It is the juice obtained from the thick fleshy leaves of a succulent plant that grows around the shores of the Indian Ocean. In the ancient world it was dissolved in

Flax

water and added to the sweet-smelling incenses used in purifying the bodies of the dead.

The linen in which Jesus was wound was made from flax, the oldest textile fiber known. The flax plant grows only about three feet in height and appears very delicate, but Near Eastern peoples early recognized its value in making a strong fabric. The stalks were laid on the roofs of houses to dry in the sun, then the fibers were separated from the stalks and spun into linen. In the ancient world there were different grades of linen. Fine linen was used in the clothes of the rich, for curtain hangings in the Temple, and even for the sails of Phoenician trading ships. The poor people, however, wore only ordinary coarse linen. The Bible did not specify that Jesus was wound in fine linen, and so we can assume that the linen of the humble people was used.

To the Romans the death of Jesus on Golgotha must have had no more significance than the deaths of the thousands of other Jews they crucified at that time. Soon, though, the whole ancient world heard about Jesus, as his disciples carried his teachings to the farthest outposts of the Roman Empire.

IX. The Last Two Thousand Years

The people of the Bible lands had cared for the earth and they made it bring forth bounty. They built reservoirs and stored water in underground cisterns, terraced the hillsides, built irrigation systems, and planted trees to stop erosion. But in the last two thousand years the cisterns and reservoirs fell into disrepair, the terraces were allowed to crumble, the forests were ruthlessly cut down, and too many sheep and goats were permitted to overgraze the vegetation.

It is a condemnation of man's tenancy that semidesert conditions now prevail over what was once known as the Fertile Crescent. The number of people it supports today is less than it was two thousand years ago under the Romans. And these ancient people probably had a higher standard of living than those inhabiting the Bible lands today.

In 1866 Mark Twain visited the Holy Land and found nothing humorous in the conditions he saw there. He wrote: "Of all the lands there are for dismal scenery, I think Palestine must be the prince. The hills are barren, they are dull of color, they are unpicturesque in shape. The valleys are unsightly deserts fringed with a feeble vegetation that has an expression about it of being sorrowful and despondent. The Dead Sea and the Sea of Galilee sleep in the midst of a vast stretch of hill and plain wherein the eye rests upon no pleasant thing, no striking object . . . It is a hopeless, dreary, heart-broken land."

The winds, the rains, the parching heat—these are much the same as in biblical times, and so man cannot accuse a changing climate. The changes are those man himself has wrought in the last two thousand years. Were Moses to attempt an exodus today, the Israelites would starve to death in Sinai. The route of Abraham through the Negeb today leads through a wasteland. A few new animals have been introduced, such as the buffalo in about the eighth century A.D., but several other native kinds have been exterminated. Gone almost completely are the cedars of Lebanon and the broad forests. The same bird species, on the whole, still fly over the Bible lands, but in many cases their numbers are sadly depleted.

A specialist on the natural history of the Holy Land was optimistic when he wrote in 1891: "Except for the disappearance of lions and wild bulls there is no change in the fauna since Biblical times." Now, only seventy-five years later, many kinds of animals have become extinct, or nearly so. Gone forever are the leopard and the red deer, nor can any bears or wild asses be found. The ostrich and the crocodile also are gone forever, and several of the most graceful gazelles and the ibex are on the verge of extinction. The drainage of swamps has made many kinds of waterfowl rare, and the birds of prey have fled to remote gorges.

Many of the same kinds of trees can still be found, but the great forests of them were all cut down long ago, either by the Romans or by the Turks and Arabs. Witness what happened to the precious balsam trees from which the balm-of-Gilead (Jeremiah 8:22, and elsewhere) was obtained. This balsam is native to southern Arabia. The Queen of Sheba brought seeds to Jerusalem and Solomon ordered it cultivated in groves at Jericho. The groves were so highly prized that the people of Jericho defended them against theft by stationing armed guards. The groves flourished until the Moslems overran Jericho in the seventh century. They neglected the trees and even cut down groves that had withstood seventeen centuries of time.

After the conquest by Rome, the Bible lands became a backwater of the Roman Empire. No longer were they a focal point for new ideas, until, during the Middle Ages, the Mohammedans erected one of the most resplendent cultures ever to appear in the Bible lands. Some of their new ideas and inventions slowly filtered into Europe through trade, but most of them were brought back to Europe by the Crusaders.

The Crusades, undertaken between the eleventh and thirteenth centuries, failed to free the Holy Land from the Turks, but they succeeded in a far different way. Instead of territory, Europeans obtained new knowledge and new products which helped awaken them from the lethargy of the Dark Ages. Paper, without which printing could not have developed, came to Europe by way of the Mohammedans. Caravans and ships brought spices from Arabia. The Arabic numerals in use today replaced the clumsy Roman system. The Arabs far surpassed Europe in the sciences of chemistry and medicine, and even many of our common terms in these sciences—such as "alkali," "elixir," and "alcohol"—were derived from Arabic words. New plants used for food and for textiles were carried back to Europe. The list of such plants is an exceedingly long one, and it includes rice, buckwheat, sugar cane, asparagus, orange, lemon, lime, apricot, hemp, and cotton.

The ancient world of biblical times has long since disappeared, but now the science of archaeology is re-creating it. Archaeologists not only excavate with shovels and pick-axes. They also use such modern tools as aerial photography, which can detect the faint outlines of buried cities, and radioactivity, which dates quite accurately pottery shards and even charcoal from fires found in ancient cities. Of all archaeological work being done in the world today, probably the most intensive is being carried on in the Bible lands. Gibeon, where once the sun stood still for Joshua's attacking army, is now uncovered. Jericho has shed new light on the life of the Canaanites. Ephesus in Turkey, where Paul preached, is yielding up its age-old secrets.

Even Armageddon, where the book of Revelations states that the last battle on earth will be fought, has been excavated. Armageddon, or *Har Megiddon* in Hebrew, means "hill of Megiddo." When it was excavated by the University of Chicago, the ruins of twenty cities, one atop the

Cotton

other, that had been built between about 4000 and 400
B.C., were discovered. It is a suitable place to imagine the
last battle taking place, since it has been one of the world's
most frequent battlegrounds.

Numerous scholars from Europe and North America
have cooperated in digging up the history of the Bible, but
much of the recent interest is due to one remarkable man,
Dr. Nelson Glueck. Dr. Glueck is president of Cincinna-

ti's Hebrew Union College, and also one of the world's most respected archaeologists. Since 1932 he has been ranging the Holy Land on camelback, accompanied only by an Arabian guide—and his copy of the Bible. To him the Bible represents an indispensable tool for seeking out lost cities, caravan routes, and details of the everyday life of biblical times. His amazing number of important archaeological discoveries is due largely to the faith he places in the Bible's accuracy about the land and its peoples. He has stated: "Scores of archaeological findings have been made which confirm in clear outline or in exact detail historical statements in the Bible."

The Bible came alive in his hands as he rode the ancient caravan routes on his camel and camped on the sites where great events narrated in the Bible took place. Around him grew many of the same kinds of plants mentioned in the Bible, and the air was filled with the same birds. Through his careful study, Dr. Glueck has been able to locate more than fifteen hundred ancient sites. He has helped to trace much of Abraham's route to the Promised Land and to date approximately when the exodus of the Israelites from Egypt took place. Bible in hand, he located the long-lost mines of Solomon at Ezion-geber and discovered the seaport to which the fleet brought ivory, apes, and peacocks. Dr. Glueck and his tireless co-workers have made the mute rocks of the Holy Land speak.

A major advance in reconstructing the biblical past was due not to a trained archaeologist but to a fifteen-year-old Bedouin shepherd. The shepherd was searching for a lost goat near the northwestern shore of the Dead Sea during the spring of 1947. There he stumbled upon the cave of Qumran, which contained pottery jars filled with decaying leather strips, sewn together into scrolls. And there was writing on these scrolls: portions of almost all of the books of the Old Testament as well as numerous commentaries written about them. Many of these texts had been stored in pottery jars, an ancient method of preserving documents, as witness Jeremiah's advice (32:14): "put them in an earthen vessel, that they may continue many days." These Dead Sea scrolls, as they are now known, survived because earthquakes and rockslides had sealed the cave against both weather and theft. One of the pottery jars at Qumran contained a copy of the book of Isaiah that may be a thousand years older than any previous text. It will take years for scholars to translate and study these fragments, but there is no doubt that eventually they will illuminate many of the events in both the Old and New Testaments.

The caves were inhabited between 110 and 31 B.C. and again between A.D. 1 and 68 by a Jewish sect, possibly the Essenes (some scholars believe that John the Baptist had been a member of this sect). The sect led a rigorously simple life, preserving its traditions against the surrounding paganism. The texts were hidden in the caves to safeguard them against the Roman soldiers who were determined to destroy Judaism and Christianity. During the dark years of the destruction of the Holy Land by the Roman legions, these pious people, huddled in their caves overlooking the barrenness around the Dead Sea, must at times have felt a deep despondency. But their faith proved not to have been misplaced.

Today the Holy Land is once again divided among nations. When the modern State of Israel, which includes most of the Holy Land, was established in 1948, the Jews did not find this Promised Land flowing with milk and honey, as had the people under Joshua. They arrived in a denuded land, half of it desert, where sand dunes lay atop what had once been fertile soil. At that time an American scientist labeled it "one of the worst eroded areas of the world."

Now, however, Israel is carrying out Isaiah's prophecy that "the desert shall blossom as the rose." The modern inhabitants of the Holy Land went right to work to restore the land. Within only ten years they had doubled the amount of land capable of being farmed. They had found underground sources of water for irrigation. Today there are vast stretches of the Holy Land where grass and trees grow instead of thorns and thistles.

More than twenty-five million trees have been planted in just one year, mostly several species of pine and also Australian eucalyptus. Early in the last century an Australian sent some eucalyptus seeds to a friend in the Holy Land with the wish: "May a mighty blessing come through these seeds." The eucalyptus has truly turned out to be a blessing, for it is an extraordinary tree of many uses. The wood of certain species is particularly strong, even rivaling iron for sturdiness in building, and it is also immune to the attack of most insects. It has been planted in swamps to help drain them, since its long leaves evaporate the tremendous amounts of water taken in by the roots. Other kinds of eucalyptus line thousands of miles of roads, serving as windbreaks.

The main guidebook to the rebuilding of the Holy Land is the Bible itself. To new settlers in Israel in 1948 it seemed hopeless to make this barren land fruitful again. Typical of what has been done all over Israel can be seen in the Negeb Desert. When Israeli scientists went to work in the Negeb, they knew that if this harsh area could be made green again, then it could be done anywhere else in the Holy Land. The scientists knew that the rainfall in the Negeb was too scant for anything to grow except thorns. Yet Abraham had found many villages there, and these villages must have been able to obtain water for crops. The Bible gave a hint: "And Isaac digged again the wells of water, which they had digged in the days of Abraham his father" (Genesis 26:18). The archaeologists searched in that area—and they found the wells and the pure water that had not been tapped for thousands of years. Several other wells that are mentioned in the book of Genesis have been located and today supply water for Israeli settlements.

There was no end of other hints for restoring the land. The Bible states that Abraham planted a tamarisk tree in Beersheba. Forestry experts decided to try planting tamarisk also. The trees flourished, for this is one of the few species that can survive in an area of such low rainfall. I recently saw tens of thousands of tamarisks planted in the vicinity of Beer-sheba, all the result of a hint from Abraham.

The Bible also seems to speak of using dew for farming. At first this was thought to be a mistranslation, but archaeologists have discovered, in practically waterless places in the Negeb, circular stone walls that apparently were used for collecting dew. Each wall seems to have been a device to make use of the principle of condensation. When the desert winds blow through a chink in the wall, the moisture they carry is deposited inside the circle of stones. That is where ancient farmers planted an olive tree or a vine, one plant to each stone circle. Now we can understand the passage in the Bible that states that Jacob sucked "honey out of the rock, and oil out of the flinty rock" (Deuteronomy 32:13). The juice of the grape was honey and the oil was the product of olive trees. Nowadays some modern farmers in the deserts of Israel follow the ancient practice of building dew collectors.

Modern Israelis are learning how to fight the desert from the ancient Nabataeans, water experts who moved northward from Arabia into the Negeb and flourished between about the third century B.C. and the second century A.D. The civilization the Nabataeans erected was based on their mastery of irrigation and water storage. Practically every river gives evidence of the dams, terraces, spillways, and aqueducts they built. They learned to divert water from the hills, to catch it in cisterns carved out of rock, to spread it over their fields. By the use of these skills, the Nabataeans created an empire out of a seemingly waterless desert.

I visited one of these ancient Nabataean farms in the Negeb Desert. It was built more than two thousand years ago by Nabataeans, and now it has been reconstructed along its original lines by Professor Michael Evenari of the Department of Botany of Hebrew University. Professor Evenari is growing those plants indigenous to the Negeb exactly the way the Israelites and the Nabataeans grew them, and using the same water conservation methods. He has restored the intricate system of dams and channels that catches the winter floods and stores the waters for summer use. The terraces were rebuilt on their ancient foundations, and even the stone fences around the farms have been restored. The scientists have already learned one important fact: it is possible to make the Negeb blossom again, using native plants and ancient techniques.

It would be impractical to try to bring back the ostrich or the bear or the lion, but it is both practical and necessary to make the cradle of civilization blossom once more. As I stood on the hillside Nabataean farm, green and luxuriant, and looked out on the yellow wastes of the Negeb, I could not help thinking that here something major had been accomplished in restoring the Bible lands.

X. Suggested Readings

A vast literature exists about the geography, wildlife, plants, and peoples of the Bible lands. Most of it, though, is highly technical, specialized as to subject matter, or in foreign languages. This is the first book that has attempted to gather much of this information and to present it for the general reader. More specific information than it has been possible to give in the short space of this book can sometimes be found in the readings listed below. The list is divided into two categories: books that can be understood by anyone who has already read this book; and more specialized books that place greater demands of attention and information on the reader.

GENERAL BOOKS

All the Birds of the Bible by Alice Parmalee. New York, Harper & Row, 1959.

All the Plants of the Bible by Winifred Walker. New York, Harper & Row, 1957.

The Animals in the Bible by Roy Pinney. Philadelphia, Chilton, 1964.

Bible Animals: Mammals of the Bible by Lulu R. Wiley. New York, Vantage Press, 1957.

The Bible as History by Werner Keller. New York, Morrow, revised edition, 1964.

Bible Plants for American Gardens by Eleanor A. King. New York, Macmillan, 1941.

Everyday Life in Old Testament Times by E. W. Heaton. New York, Scribner's, 1956.

The Golden Bible Atlas by Samuel Terrien. New York, Golden Press, 1959.

Landscapes of the Bible by George Eichholz. New York, Harper & Row, 1963.

A Naturalist in Palestine by Victor Howells. London, Andrew Melrose, Ltd., 1956.

Plants of the Bible by A. W. Anderson. London, Crosby Lockwood & Son, 1956.

Shorter Atlas of the Bible by L. H. Grollenberg. New York, Nelson, 1959.

Story of the Bible World by Nelson B. Keyes. Pleasantville, New York, The Reader's Digest Association, 1962.

This Is the Holy Land by Fulton J. Sheen, H. V. Morton, and Yousuf Karsh, New York, Doubleday, Image Books, 1962.

ADVANCED BOOKS

Animal and Man in Bible Lands by F. S. Bodenheimer. Leiden, Netherlands, E. J. Brill, 1960.

The Archaeology of Palestine by W. F. Albright. Baltimore, Penguin Books, revised edition, 1961.

The Biblical Archaeologist Reader edited by G. Ernest Wright and David N. Freedman. New York, Doubleday, Anchor Books, 1961.

The Biblical Archaeologist Reader 2 edited by E. F. Campbell, Jr. and David N. Freedman. New York, Doubleday, Anchor Books, 1964.

The Canaanites by John Gray. New York, Praeger, 1964.

The Dead Sea Scrolls: An Introduction by R. K. Harrison. New York, Harper & Row, Torchbooks, 1961.

The Geography of the Bible by Dennis Baly. New York, Harper & Row, 1957.

The Geography of Israel by Efraim Orni and Elisha Efrat. Jerusalem, Israel Program for Scientific Translations, 1964.

The Medes and the Persians by W. Culican. New York, Praeger, 1965.

The Phoenicians by Donald Harden. New York, Praeger, 1962.

Plants of the Bible by Harold N. Moldenke. New York, Ronald Press, 1952.

Rivers in the Desert: A History of the Negev by Nelson Glueck. New York, Farrar, Straus, 1959.

Through Lands of the Bible by H. V. Morton. New York, Dodd, Mead, 1938.

The World of the Old Testament by Cyrus H. Gordon. New York, Doubleday, 1958.

XI. Index of Biblical References

XII. Subject Index

Format by Carolyn Voigt and Gloria Bressler
Set in 12 pt. Garamond Linotype
Composed by The Haddon Craftsmen
Printed by Murray Printing Company
Bound by Haddon Bindery
HARPER & ROW, PUBLISHERS, INCORPORATED

520808   Farb, P.

Land, wildlife, and peoples of
                              the Bible
220.8 F219

Salt Lake County Public Library System
Headquarters -- Midvale, Utah 84047

RULES

1. Books may be kept two weeks, and may be re-
newed for the same period. Magazines circulate for one
week.

2. A fine of two cents a day will be charged on
each item which is not returned according to the above
rule. Nothing will be issued to any person incurring
such a fine until it has been paid.

3. All injuries to materials, beyond reasonable wear,
and all losses shall be made good.

4. Each borrower is held responsible for all items
drawn on his plate and for all fines accruing on the
same.